Battered Women

OTHER BOOKS OF RELATED INTEREST

OPPOSING VIEWPOINTS SERIES
America's Victims
Child Abuse
Child Welfare
Crime and Criminals
Gun Control
Human Rights
Islam
Male/Female Roles
Pornography
Sexual Values
Sexual Violence
Violence
Working Women

CURRENT CONTROVERSIES SERIES
Gay Rights
Family Violence
Marriage and Divorce
Violence Against Women
Youth Violence

AT ISSUE SERIES
Domestic Violence
Rape on Campus
What Is Sexual Harassment?

Battered Women

Louise Gerdes, *Book Editor*

David L. Bender, *Publisher*
Bruno Leone, *Executive Editor*
Bonnie Szumski, *Editorial Director*
Brenda Stalcup, *Managing Editor*
Scott Barbour, *Senior Editor*

Contemporary Issues
Companion

Greenhaven Press, Inc., San Diego, CA

Library of Congress Cataloging-in-Publication Data

Battered women / Louise Gerdes, book editor.
    p.   cm. — (Contemporary issues companion)
    Includes bibliographical references and index.
    ISBN 1-56510-896-5 (pbk. : alk. paper). —
ISBN 1-56510-897-3 (lib. : alk. paper)
    1. Abused women. 2. Abused wives. 3. Wife abuse. I. Gerdes,
Louise. II. Series
HV1444.B37 1999
362.82'92—dc21   98-27299
                                                     CIP

©1999 by Greenhaven Press, Inc.
P.O. Box 289009, San Diego, CA 92198-9009

Printed in the U.S.A.

CONTENTS

FOREWORD

In the news, on the streets, and in neighborhoods, individuals are confronted with a variety of social problems. Such problems may affect people directly: A young woman may struggle with depression, suspect a friend of having bulimia, or watch a loved one battle cancer. And even the issues that do not directly affect her private life—such as religious cults, domestic violence, or legalized gambling—still impact the larger society in which she lives. Discovering and analyzing the complexities of issues that encompass communal and societal realms as well as the world of personal experience is a valuable educational goal in the modern world.

Effectively addressing social problems requires familiarity with a constantly changing stream of data. Becoming well informed about today's controversies is an intricate process that often involves reading myriad primary and secondary sources, analyzing political debates, weighing various experts' opinions—even listening to first-hand accounts of those directly affected by the issue. For students and general observers, this can be a daunting task because of the sheer volume of information available in books, periodicals, on the evening news, and on the Internet. Researching the consequences of legalized gambling, for example, might entail sifting through congressional testimony on gambling's societal effects, examining private studies on Indian gaming, perusing numerous websites devoted to Internet betting, and reading essays written by lottery winners as well as interviews with recovering compulsive gamblers. Obtaining valuable information can be time-consuming—since it often requires researchers to pore over numerous documents and commentaries before discovering a source relevant to their particular investigation.

Greenhaven's Contemporary Issues Companion series seeks to assist this process of research by providing readers with useful and pertinent information about today's complex issues. Each volume in this anthology series focuses on a topic of current interest, presenting informative and thought-provoking selections written from a wide variety of viewpoints. The readings selected by the editors include such diverse sources as personal accounts and case studies, pertinent factual and statistical articles, and relevant commentaries and overviews. This diversity of sources and views, found in every Contemporary Issues Companion, offers readers a broad perspective in one convenient volume.

In addition, each title in the Contemporary Issues Companion series is designed especially for young adults. The selections included in every volume are chosen for their accessibility and are expertly edited in consideration of both the reading and comprehension levels of the audience. The structure of the anthologies also enhances accessibility. An introductory essay places each issue in context and provides helpful facts such as historical background or current statistics and legislation that pertain to the topic. The chapters that follow organize the material and focus on specific aspects of the book's topic. Every essay is introduced by a brief summary of its main points and biographical information about the author. These summaries aid in comprehension and can also serve to direct readers to material of immediate interest and need. Finally, a comprehensive index allows readers to efficiently scan and locate content.

The Contemporary Issues Companion series is an ideal launching point for research on a particular topic. Each anthology in the series is composed of readings taken from an extensive gamut of resources, including periodicals, newspapers, books, government documents, the publications of private and public organizations, and Internet websites. In these volumes, readers will find factual support suitable for use in reports, debates, speeches, and research papers. The anthologies also facilitate further research, featuring a book and periodical bibliography and a list of organizations to contact for additional information.

A perfect resource for both students and the general reader, Greenhaven's Contemporary Issues Companion series is sure to be a valued source of current, readable information on social problems that interest young adults. It is the editors' hope that readers will find the Contemporary Issues Companion series useful as a starting point to formulate their own opinions about and answers to the complex issues of the present day.

INTRODUCTION

Domestic violence represents a serious and long-standing problem in the United States as well as many other parts of the world. Domestic violence can take place between partners of the same sex, and men are sometimes battered by their female partners. However, in the vast majority of cases, the victims are women who are battered by their male partners or former partners. In fact, statistics show that women are ten times more likely than men to be victims of domestic violence. Furthermore, the number of women who are battered is high: Four million incidents of domestic violence against women are reported every year. These statistics are based on crime survey estimates that rely largely on FBI, police, and emergency room medical reports. However, many women report domestic violence to friends, family, relatives, clergy, physicians, and nurses—sources not reflected in crime surveys. Therefore, the number of battered women may be even greater than crime surveys reveal.

Anna Quindlen, a Pulitzer Prize–winning columnist, has called domestic violence "the quiet crime." Until recently, few people in America were aware of the domestic violence occurring all around them, even when it affected other family members or close friends. Nor did they realize the widespread nature and extent of family abuse in their communities. According to Robert L. Snow, a police captain in Indianapolis, Indiana, "Even those of us who work regularly with the victims and perpetrators of family abuse know only of the cases that come to our attention, but no one really knows how many victims of physical, sexual, emotional, and financial abuse simply suffer in silence, and never come to the attention of anyone outside their immediate family."

People rarely have an accurate picture of the typical battered woman. Often, they think of battered women as stay-at-home mothers from working-class or poor families. However, statistics show that battering is a phenomenon that affects women of all income levels, occupations, cultures, races, and ages. "In this country," Donna E. Shalala, the secretary of the U.S. Department of Health and Human Services, remarks, "domestic violence is just about as common as giving birth."

People also have difficulty visualizing the typical batterer. Many people assume that batterers are poorly educated, lower-class brutes. "We somehow expect that hurtful people will look the part," suggests batterer treatment program therapist Donald G. Dutton, "They're not one of us—and especially not one of our heroes." The inaccuracy of this belief was driven home to many Americans in 1994 as they listened to 911 tapes of Nicole Brown Simpson pleading for help while her ex-husband, O.J. Simpson—an amiable and well-liked professional football star, sports commentator, and comedic actor—raged, cursed, and broke down the door in the background. The tapes were made public after the 1994 murders of Nicole and her friend Ron Goldman. In October 1995, O.J. Simpson was acquitted of these murders, but he was found liable for their deaths in a 1997 civil trial decision. Media accounts continue to reveal allegations that revered public figures— including actors, musicians, athletes, and public officials—have abused their intimate partners.

Historically, society's attitude toward the problem of domestic violence has influenced the way the legal system has responded to it. In the eighteenth century, the predominant belief maintained that a wife was essentially the property of her husband; if she defied his authority, he was legally entitled to subject her to physical "chastisement." In the nineteenth century, such punishment became the subject of widespread controversy. Experts argued that force was an ineffective method of instilling authority. Furthermore, the temperance and women's rights movements that began in the nineteenth century challenged the validity of a husband's right to beat his wife. However, domestic violence was still considered to be a private family matter as opposed to a criminal act. Although by the 1870s there was no judge in the United States who recognized a husband's legal right to beat his wife, the courts tended to grant men accused of wife beating a variety of formal and informal immunities from prosecution. "The American legal system continued to treat wife beating differently from other cases of assault and battery," writes law professor Reva B. Shargel. "While authorities denied that a husband had the right to beat his wife, they intervened only intermittently in cases of marital violence . . . in order to promote 'domestic harmony.'" Even at the turn of the twentieth century, formal prosecution of abusers was not considered appropriate; courts and prosecutors believed that rehabilitation should be the primary goal and that the interactions within a family should remain private.

In the late 1970s, the feminist movement began to challenge the concept of family privacy that shielded wife abuse, and since then, it has secured many reforms designed to protect women from domestic violence. During the last two decades, the legal system has faced pressure from both inside and outside to protect women from violence. However, it was not until 1991 that the problem of domestic abuse attracted the attention of legislators in Washington, D.C.

In response to legislation proposed in 1991 by Senator Joseph R. Biden, Congress began to hear testimony from women's rights and civil rights organizations, state attorneys general, law professors, law enforcement officials, physicians, and victims of violence. Testimony at the legislative hearings indicated that it was necessary to address domestic violence committed against women because many state laws failed to provide these victims with the "equal protection of the laws" mandated by the Fourteenth Amendment of the U.S. Constitution. In 1991, only seventeen states kept data on reported domestic violence offenses. Although injuries that battered women receive are at least as serious as injuries suffered in 90 percent of violent felony crimes, under state laws, battering was almost always classified as a misdemeanor. Many state policies and procedures restricted the prosecution of domestic violence, which discouraged prosecutors from pursuing domestic violence cases. In addition, the congressional hearings showed that discriminatory administrative procedures, including insensitive and unresponsive treatment by police, prosecutors, and judges, often resulted in low reporting and conviction rates.

From the expert testimony given at the congressional hearings emerged a comprehensive statute containing a wide range of provisions designed to address the problem of violence against women. This statute gradually evolved into the Violence Against Women Act, which was signed into law by President Bill Clinton in September 1994 as part of an anti-crime bill. Generally, the act combined tough federal penalties with substantial resources to the states and communities for the training of law enforcement officers and prosecutors to better identify and respond to violent crimes against women, including domestic violence.

In an effort to achieve equal justice for women in the courts, the act authorizes grants to train judges, law officers, and prosecutors to more effectively prevent, identify, and respond to domestic violence crimes. Because investigating domestic violence cases is significantly different from investigating other crimes, the Justice Department incorporates into the training an understanding of the life of a battered woman both emotionally and contextually. For example, victims of domestic violence often recant their charges because they are afraid and in danger, and knowledge of this fact enables criminal justice officials to better handle such situations. "It's easy to get frustrated with battered women if you don't know what's really happening in their lives," remarks Bonnie Campbell, director of the Justice Department's Violence Against Women Office. "Very few of us live believing that the person we're sharing our home with might well kill us. That's a pretty horrifying environment by anyone's definition." Campbell contends that once members of the criminal justice system more fully understand the situations typically faced by battered women, they can become as supportive of these victims as they would be of any other set of victims.

The Violence Against Women Act also criminalizes interstate domestic violence. As of 1994, it became a federal crime, punishable by up to five years in prison, for anyone to cross state lines to do bodily injury to a spouse or intimate partner. Batterers who cross state lines can be sentenced to prison for up to ten years if they use dangerous weapons, up to twenty if they cause life-threatening injuries, and to life in prison if they kill their victims. This section of the law has already produced results. For example, Derek Page brutally beat his former girlfriend with a hammer, then drove her more than a hundred miles from Ohio to Pennsylvania where he left her at a hospital. He did so because he hoped to avoid Ohio's arrest policy in domestic violence cases. However, because of the new law, Page was convicted in April 1996 by the southern district court of Ohio. Unfortunately, as of 1998, these new provisions have not been utilized to any great extent. The Justice Department reports that since 1994, U.S. attorneys have only undertaken thirty-seven prosecutions under the act's criminal provisions, which amounts to barely more than one per month for the entire nation. "Laws are meaningless without vigorous enforcement—and there is still very little of that," according to George Lardner, Jr., whose daughter was murdered in 1992 by her ex-boyfriend.

The act also addresses the inconsistent statistics on the actual number of women who are battered. For example, the Uniform Crime Reports estimates four million incidents of domestic violence each year, while the National Crime Victimization Survey indicates an annual five million violent victimizations of women twelve and older. The Bureau of Justice Statistics has found that the incidence of domestic violence may be four times greater than the National Crime Victimization Survey indicates. Therefore, the Violence Against Women Act specifically mandated a massive research effort on the actual extent of violent acts against women. As of January 1998, this survey was in the process of being conducted by the National Institute of Justice and the National Academy of Sciences.

The most controversial and far-reaching section of the act has been the Civil Rights Remedies for Gender-Motivated Violence provision, which states that "all persons within the United States shall have the right to be free from crimes of violence motivated by gender." This provision allows victims of gender-motivated violence to sue their attackers in civil court and collect monetary damages. Some legal authorities warned that the remedy would "flood" the courts with claims, while others argued that it was unconstitutional. By the spring of 1998, only seven women had sued their attackers under this provision. In six of these cases, federal district judges ruled that the provision was constitutional and that Congress does have the authority to pass a law that allows women this kind of relief. Campbell sees the civil rights remedy as essential: "It is the fundamental right of every woman to live her life free of violence—it's a civil right, a human right."

Efforts to make the lives of women safe continue. On May 21, 1998, Senators Paul Wellstone, Joe Biden, and Arlen Specter introduced to Congress a second Violence Against Women Act. Wellstone said that the proposed legislation "is a public recognition that, for too many women, the home, rather than being a safe place, can be a very dangerous place." Public awareness of the existence and extent of domestic violence constitutes an important step toward eradicating it. The authors in *Battered Women: Contemporary Issues Companion* explore the nature and scope of this serious problem as well as possible solutions.

CHAPTER 1

THE NATURE OF VIOLENCE OF VIOLENCE AGAINST WOMEN

Contemporary Issues
Companion

TWO PERSPECTIVES ON DOMESTIC VIOLENCE

Loretta J. Stalans and Arthur J. Lurigio

Loretta J. Stalans and Arthur J. Lurigio, professors of criminal justice at Loyola University in Chicago, discuss two theoretical perspectives concerning the causes of domestic violence and how these different theories lead to different approaches to solving the problem. According to the authors, the family violence perspective proposes that men and women from violent families are equally violent; therefore, this theory focuses on solutions that identify individual batterers and provide them with treatment. The feminist perspective, the authors write, holds that societal attitudes and beliefs subordinating women foster domestic violence. Stalans and Lurigio explain that solutions arising from the feminist perspective include giving police broader power to arrest batterers and providing shelters where victims receive support, counseling, and a safe place to live.

In 1995, the public was reminded that domestic violence against women has no racial or social class boundaries. Nicole Brown Simpson knew firsthand that wealthy Caucasian women are beaten and psychologically abused. The O.J. Simpson trial [in which Simpson was acquitted in October 1995 of the murder of his ex-wife, Nicole Brown Simpson, and her friend, Ronald Goldman] dramatically portrays the terror of a battered woman's life and considers the question of whether Nicole Brown Simpson is yet another victim of domestic murder—a fatal consequence that happens all too often in America. According to the National Crime Victimization Survey (NCVS), women are 10 times more likely than men to be victims of violence inflicted by their intimate partners. Based on a national survey of reported incidents of violence (from slapping to choking or using a weapon), Murray Straus estimated that "over 6 million women are beaten every year in the United States. This is a lower bound estimate and the true figure easily could be double that."

About 1.8 million women experience at least one of the more serious forms of violence, such as being kicked, punched, choked, or

From Loretta J. Stalans and Arthur J. Lurigio, "Responding to Domestic Violence Against Women," *Crime and Delinquency*, vol. 41, no. 4, October 1995, pp. 387–98. Copyright ©1995 by Sage Publications, Inc. Reprinted by permission of Sage Publications, Inc.

attacked with a weapon. These numbers, of course, are just estimates because all data sources either underestimate or overestimate certain forms of violence. Women experience similar risks of violence in urban, suburban, and rural areas. Ethnic or racial background is unrelated to rates of violence in the home, but age and social class do place women at a higher risk for violent attacks: younger women with less education and lower incomes have much higher rates of victimizations by intimates than do older women and women with more education and higher incomes.

Women are more likely than men to be seriously injured in domestic violence incidents, as documented by police records and victimization surveys such as Lisa P. Brush's nationwide survey of 5,474 U.S. households in 1988. Brush asked males and females in married couples the following: "Have you ever been cut, bruised, or seriously injured in a fight with your partner?" "Has your partner ever been cut, bruised, or seriously injured?" Women reported that they were hurt more often than their partners. Moreover, in situations where both partners were violent, women were more likely to be seriously injured. Data from emergency rooms, police reports, and court records also support the conclusion that in domestic disputes women receive more serious injuries than men. However, men are less likely to report victimization experiences, and many incidents of domestic violence, whether women or men are victims, never come to the attention of police or physicians.

The Consequences of Domestic Violence

As the above findings clearly suggest, women are susceptible to repeat victimizations in the home and may become hopelessly entangled in abusive relationships. They fear not only the consequences of staying but also, and even more, the consequences of leaving those relationships. In the NCVS, 20% of women reported that they had been victims of intimate violence at least three times in the prior 6 months. Many women do not react passively and helplessly when faced with repeat abuse. Most seek help from family, friends, or government agencies. In the NCVS, about 80% attempted to defend themselves: 40% reasoned with the offenders and 40% used physical force. More than one half of the women who attempted to protect themselves thought that their tactics had helped, whereas one fourth believed that their tactics had worsened the situations. Faced with repeated abuse, women often begin to anticipate the next violent episode and may engage in behaviors to actually trigger the violence; for them, the anticipation of abuse is often worse than the abuse itself. Victims of violent street crimes typically do not have contact with offenders after the crime; in contrast, domestic violence victims and their perpetrators often share children, property, insurance, and homes. Even if victims leave their homes, courts often force them to allow offenders to visit their children. Victims of domestic violence are particularly vulnerable to repeat abuse because their children make it difficult to sever all contacts with offenders.

The most fatal consequence of domestic violence frequently happens after escalating incidents of repeat violence. The exact number of homicides that occur because of the actions of intimates is difficult to estimate because the nature of the relationships between victims and offenders is often unknown (e.g., 39% of the relationships were unknown in FBI data for 1992). Based on FBI data from 1977 to 1992, an estimated 1,432 women and 657 men were killed by intimates in 1992. The ratio of women to men who kill their intimate partners varies by race. In 1977, a greater number of African American women killed their husbands compared to African American men who killed their wives, but by 1992 a greater number of African American men killed their wives. According to Marianne W. Zawitz, "Among Whites, wives have always outnumbered husbands as victims of intimate murder." More than half of the victims and offenders were drinking alcohol at the time of the murders. Several studies report that in instances where wives killed their husbands, the husbands were the first to use physical force or to threaten the use of a weapon. In 1991, 70% of women prisoners incarcerated for intimate violence were first-time offenders, compared to only 30% of men incarcerated for intimate violence. Of those incarcerated for intimate violence, men with previous convictions for violent crimes outnumbered women almost 3 to 1.

Two Perspectives on Domestic Violence

Why does domestic violence occur and what can society and the criminal justice system do about it? Demie Kurz described two theoretical perspectives that have dominated domestic violence research: the family violence perspective and the feminist perspective. For the family violence perspective, the unit of analysis is the family. For the feminist perspective, the unit of analysis is the relationship between men and women; it encompasses all forms of violence against women from sexual harassment in the workplace to physical, verbal, and sexual abuse in the home. Both perspectives urge the legal system to focus on violence against women, but they do so for different reasons, which lead to different solutions to the problem.

The family violence perspective maintains that women and men are equally likely to engage in violence, as evidenced by survey data showing that women and men report similar incidences of physical violence against their partners. Straus and colleagues found that about 12% of men and women in their study sample engaged in violence and that in 49% of the homes where violence occurred, both men and women were perpetrators. Other surveys have replicated the finding that men and women report similar levels of violence. Feminists criticize these results by pointing out that many of women's acts of physical aggression are actually attempts to defend themselves from men's attacks. According to NCVS data, twice as many women physically attacked intimate assailants to protect themselves than attacked stranger assailants for self-protection (40% vs. 20%, respectively). Feminists point to the higher percentages of women victims of violence (as opposed to women perpetrators) in police and court records, emergency room data, and victimization surveys to underscore the fact that women are much more likely to be victims of domestic violence.

The family violence perspective suggests that women and men learn from childhood experiences and from media portrayals and societal norms that violence is an acceptable way to resolve disputes. In the family violence perspective, therefore, domestic violence is no different from other forms of violence such as stranger-on-stranger violence and violence against children, the elderly, and other social groups—all of which are seen to result from faulty socialization. The family violence perspective focuses on women victims because men engage in more dangerous forms of violence that lead to more serious injuries.

The Feminist Perspective

Feminists argue that male dominance is a central component in understanding why domestic violence occurs and in finding solutions to it. Feminists assert that men and women do not have equal positions in society. Men have had privileged positions in society for centuries and have acquired and maintained these positions by keeping women subordinate. According to this viewpoint, organized religion has perpetuated the attitudes and beliefs that lead to violence against women and children. As Kurz observed:

> Feminists believe that the decontextualized family violence perspective denies a central element of women's experience by deflecting attention from one of the key places where women's oppression occurs—in the family. For feminists, family violence is a direct outcome of men's attempt to maintain control over the powerless members of the family—women and children.

Because it ignores variables such as social structure and gender, the family violence perspective places great importance on psychological problems of individuals and families. Michelle Fine discussed the implications of concentrating on individuals rather than on the gender-based nature of violence:

> To focus on the individual . . . contributes to a discourse that finally blames individual survivors, for the source of social inequity is sought inside their bodies and minds. Not only does such an approach decontextualize a woman from her

political, social, and personal worlds, but it systematically ren-
ders oblique the structure of patriarchy, racism, and classism,
and advanced capitalism that have sculpted what appear to be
the "conditions" or "choices" of her life.

History supports the feminists' position that laws and community
norms perpetuate violence against women. The U.S. Constitution
declares that "all men are created equal," but did not extend human
and civil rights to women until several decades after its passage. In the
17th and 18th centuries, women were property that could be bought
and sold, and they were disciplined through physical punishment.
Women did not have the right to own property, to vote, or to manage
their wages. According to R. Emerson Dobash and Russell Dobash:

> Married women had always been controlled and abused by
> legal loss of their property upon marriage and by the husband's
> right to exploit their labor and to appropriate their wages, but
> the Married Women's Property Act of 1857 forbade a husband
> to "seize his wife's earnings and neglect her and allowed her to
> keep her own wages after the desertion of her lord."

Historical Views of Domestic Violence

Until the 19th century, husbands who beat their wives could use the
defense of chastisement. In the latter part of the 19th century, domestic violence was considered a crime and laws were created to punish
offenders at the whipping post. "Courts declared that 'the rule of love
superseded the rule of force' and 'the moral sense of the community
revolts at the idea that the husband may inflict personal chastisement
upon his wife, even for the most outrageous conduct,'" stated Dobash
and Dobash. These laws, however, were rarely enforced.

At the turn of the 20th century, domestic violence was viewed once
again as a "private matter" that should be kept out of public view.
Many states created statutes that did not allow police officers to arrest
perpetrators for domestic violence misdemeanors where a neutral
third party did not witness the episode. Courts and prosecutors
believed that formal prosecution was not appropriate and that rehabilitation was the goal. Historically, legal statutes, criminal justice
authorities, and community members have regarded violence against
women in the home as a "private matter of the family," best handled
through advice or mediation.

During the last two decades, the legal system has faced inside and
outside pressure to protect women from violence. The women's
movement in the 1970s focused on violence against women and characterized the problem as a public concern. Civil liability suits filed
against police departments for failing to provide equal protection to
women injured in domestic violence incidents signaled to all law

enforcement agencies that ignoring battered women can lead to litigation and financial losses. Academic research also called attention to
the problems of existing domestic violence policies. For example,
research shows that the likelihood of future domestic violence is lower when police arrest batterers in domestic disputes; however, other
research suggests that the effectiveness of arrest is contingent on a
number of situational factors and batterer characteristics. Together,
feminism, court cases, and empirical findings have helped to change
state laws to give police officers more power to arrest suspects in
domestic violence incidents.

Arrest Policies Vary

Several states have changed their laws to allow police officers to arrest
suspects without victims' consent when there is probable cause.
Despite these statutory changes, only a few states actually require officers to arrest suspects under specific circumstances, such as when
there are injured victims. Officers still exercise a lot of discretion when
deciding to arrest suspects, even in states with laws mandating arrest,
because the concept of probable cause is quite ambiguous. Officers
have especially difficult times interpreting domestic violence situations where the wife and husband offer conflicting accounts of how
the injuries occurred. To handle these situations, some states have
passed laws requiring officers to determine who is the primary aggressor in an incident. In one state with a primary aggressor clause, experienced officers are rarely able to untangle the past to assess blamewor-
thiness; instead, they base their decisions to arrest on the respective
credibility and dangerousness of wives and husbands. Their "disinter-
ested objectivity," however, has still created a bias toward less formal
processing of cases involving women who violate social norms by
exhibiting symptoms of mental illness or alcoholism. Moreover,
mandatory and presumptive arrest policies have not resulted in equal
protection under the law.

Early evaluations of how legislative changes influenced local criminal justice practices suggested that gatekeepers (i.e., police officers and
prosecutors) often fail to process domestic violence cases through the
formal criminal justice system and prefer alternatives such as court-
ordered mediation. Moreover, evaluations showing higher rates of
arrest after the implementation of presumptive arrest policies did not
examine several key issues, for example, victims' satisfaction with how
the police and system treated them, whether certain groups of women
obtained less protection, whether states' attorneys lessened or dropped
the charges, and how the courts deal with convicted batterers.

Preferred arrest policies do result in significantly more arrests when
they are part of a coordinated response involving the legal system
and community agencies. Key criminal justice institutions (i.e.,
police, the prosecutor's office, courts, and defense attorneys), commu-

nity services (i.e., battered women's shelters, children's services, welfare agencies, and mental health services), and public support can change officers' decisions about using arrest as a solution to domestic violence incidents.

Prosecution Policies Are Changing

Researchers have paid relatively little attention to how domestic violence cases are prosecuted. In the past, prosecutors typically required victims of domestic violence to sign complaints against batterers, whereas prosecutors themselves signed complaints in other crimes. Prosecutors' offices are changing their procedures so that they now sign complaints against defendants, and victims serve as key witnesses in those cases; this change sends the message that domestic violence is a crime against the state. Prosecutors' offices also have adopted policies to prevent victims from dropping charges and regularly use subpoena power to force victims to appear in court. Subpoena power may prevent victims from becoming targets of retaliatory violence because victims can show that they were forced to participate in court proceedings. Prosecutors also have been successful at prosecuting cases without the participation of victims.

Research on the effectiveness of different prosecution strategies has been sparse. David A. Ford and Mary Jean Regoli concluded that

> the limited evidence on the effectiveness of alternative prosecution policies for preventing wife assault suggests that no single policy commonly advocated is better than another. The chance of a man assaulting his partner again in the short term is essentially unaffected by whether he is prosecuted under policies calling for harsh punishment or for rehabilitative treatment. What matters is that he faces treatment.

When victims initiate complaints, they are less likely to be harmed by offenders when prosecutors allow the victims to drop charges than when other strategies such as diversion or "no-drop" policies are used. This effectiveness, however, remains to be documented more thoroughly and may not generalize to police-initiated charges.

Many jurisdictions, thanks largely to the feminist perspective, have created victims' programs that help victims with their decisions to participate in the legal process and to leave domestic batterers. Several studies have found that these programs increase victims' willingness to participate in the criminal justice process as well as increase their satisfaction with the process. Few studies, however, have examined whether victim advocate programs reduce the risk that victims will experience retaliatory violence, increase their knowledge about the system and community-based programs, and empower them to take control over their lives. Research is sorely needed to better understand how interventions can assist victims' recovery and readjustment. In addressing these issues, researchers should explore the independent and combined effects of victims' programs, civil protection orders, and prosecution and sentencing strategies on victims' satisfaction, safety, recovery, and control over their lives.

Focusing on the Batterer

The family violence perspective is more likely than the feminist perspective to pay attention to the perpetrators of domestic violence. The family violence perspective, for example, encourages researchers to classify offenders into different profiles based on backgrounds and personality characteristics. Daniel G. Saunders identified three prominent risk factors for wife assault. Men are more likely to batter women if the men were abused as children. The risk of wife assault increases when both partners were abused or witnessed abuse as children. Alcohol abuse and low income are also prominent risk factors. Other risk factors include offender deficits in communication skills, rigid stereotypes of male and female roles, personality disorders, and problems with anger control. These risk factors have been used to customize treatments for batterers. Many criminal justice systems now impose court-mandated treatment at both pre- and postsentencing. In pretrial diversion programs, for example, offenders who successfully complete treatment have their arrest records cleared. Court-mandated treatment also can be part of sentences for convicted offenders.

A variety of community services and treatment programs exist to assist victims of domestic violence and to treat domestic violence offenders. Feminists have focused on the task of empowering women to control their own lives and have created social services that allow women with limited financial means to leave abusive partners and to find havens from retaliatory violence. Feminists were volunteers for the first battered women's shelters and have fought to limit the amount of funds that are diverted away from abused women to treat abusive men. Shelters provide a safe place to live and offer supportive counseling, child care, and advocacy services. The number of shelters has grown from 0 in 1970 to more than 1,300 in 1989; nonetheless, there are not enough shelters to meet the demand for services.

The effectiveness of shelters as a means of allowing women to leave violent relationships is uncertain. Research indicates that each additional step that a victim takes to seek help reduces the number of subsequent victimization incidents. Battered women can also receive counseling services from outpatient community mental health treatment programs, clergy, private counseling agencies, and women's groups, the latter of which battered women rate as more effective than the other types of counseling services.

Cultural Explanations for Domestic Violence

Marilyn Gardner

Immigrants to the United States, Marilyn Gardner writes, often have lenient attitudes toward domestic violence due to cultural values that differ from mainstream American values. In some countries of origin, Gardner explains, domestic violence is not considered a crime; immigrants from these countries often view family violence as a private matter, discouraging battered women from discussing personal matters with strangers. The author also points out that in many Asian cultures, abused women believe they have failed as wives and are hesitant to make their shame public by reporting the abuse. To reach abused women from cultures with values that tolerate domestic violence, Gardner reports, some shelters offer workshops where representatives from the battered women's culture of origin speak about their own experiences and how they changed their own attitudes. Marilyn Gardner is a staff writer for the *Christian Science Monitor*.

After Boston Red Sox outfielder Wilfredo Cordero was arrested in June 1997 for allegedly beating his wife, Ana, his first wife, Wanda Mora, offered a cultural explanation.

Ms. Mora, who said she was also abused by Mr. Cordero, explained that her former husband grew up in the housing projects of Puerto Rico. A Puerto Rican herself, she did not condone his behavior. But she described the projects as a macho environment where men and women alike often accepted domestic violence as normal.

Immigrant Views of Domestic Violence Differ

As Americans deal with domestic abuse more openly, some immigrants' view of family violence as nobody else's business—beyond the reach of social agencies—is at odds with their new cultural environment, where it is a crime. In Cordero's case, he says he did nothing wrong, and his wife says they will work out their situation.

To counselors who work with battered women and abusive men

From Marilyn Gardner, "When U.S., Newcomers' Values Clash," *The Christian Science Monitor*, July 16, 1997. Reprinted with permission from *The Christian Science Monitor*. Copyright ©1997 The Christian Science Publishing Society. All rights reserved.

from many countries, a "cultural defense" is not acceptable.

In counseling sessions, workshops, and informal talks, these workers, some of whom are from other countries themselves, are teaching immigrant women and men to reject stereotyped justifications for violence. They are also helping women to overcome the cultural sense of shame that keeps them from seeking help.

Such efforts are also taking root internationally. "In the last five to 10 years, there has been a major shift in the awareness of the international community with regard to domestic violence," says Leni Marin, program manager of the Family Violence Prevention Fund in San Francisco. "It's an exciting time. Cultural shift is happening globally on this issue."

Meanwhile, Debra Robbin, director of education and training at Casa Myrna Vazquez, a shelter for Hispanic women in Boston, acknowledges that cultural norms do vary.

"For some immigrants, domestic violence was legal in their country of origin," she says. "They have no idea people can be imprisoned for it here."

In helping battered women from other cultures, Ms. Robbin adds, "We try to start with where they're at and what they believe. We tell them this is not their lot in life. But in a cultural context, it's hard, because people are often connected by families who say, 'Hey, you married him, this is what you get. Don't embarrass us. Don't say no to your husband.'"

Help becomes further complicated, Robbin says, because within the Puerto Rican community, "it's a very big step for abused women to call a hot line. Maybe they would go to a neighbor, or their church, but telling a stranger something so personal is a foreign concept."

Help for Battered Immigrant Women

To change these attitudes, counselors at the shelter offer "culturally sensitive" workshops, conducted by women from the Latina community. "When they hear information from someone from their own background, it's more effective," Robbin says.

The shelter also maintains a speakers' bureau, offering talks by Latina women who can say, "Here's my story." By connecting with the community this way, the group hopes to reach battered women who might otherwise hesitate to come forward.

In Washington, Christel Nichols, executive director of House of Ruth, a social service agency for women and children, rejects attempts to pin domestic violence on a man's cultural background. "That makes it sound as though he's the victim here," she says. "It excuses the behavior. It's almost like, 'Oh, he can't help himself.' That's kind of a racial slur to me—that if I'm of a certain nationality, I have to act a certain way."

Instead, Ms. Nichols says, she and other counselors at House of

Ruth "try to help women and children who are victimized by domestic violence to understand that no matter what socioeconomic group or culture they belong to, this is not normal. They don't deserve this, they are special. They have to focus on themselves. That typically means moving away from the person who is abusing them—physically and emotionally."

Raising Awareness Among Asian Women

Similar approaches exist in communities where Asian immigrants predominate. In June 1997, a group of Asian women's shelters in California held its first statewide conference on domestic violence.

Called "Gathering Strength," the two-day meeting brought together diverse Asian and Pacific Islander community members. Conference organizers also invited speakers from Japan, Indonesia, Samoa, the Philippines, Sri Lanka, India, Cambodia, and Fiji to share experiences and successes in dealing with family violence in their own countries.

Among Asian groups, Ms. Marin says, domestic violence produces shame. "If you are a battered woman, you feel so ashamed. It's profound shame, because you feel you have been a failure as a wife, as a mother, as a woman. You extend that to the point that if you report this, it will not only shame you, it will also shame your husband, your children, and your entire community. There's big, big pressure not to report this."

Within the Philippine community, Marin continues, the cultural value of shame "is handed down even to those who have been born in the United States." Women's advocates are working to redefine shame, she says, adding, "Who should feel shameful is not the battered woman, but the community that doesn't support her and help her out. That's shameful."

Shame also plays a role in strategies being developed by domestic violence groups in India. In very impoverished neighborhoods of New Delhi, Marin says, "Women know it's futile to call the police, because they would never come to that part of the city. So women's advocates have banded together to publicly shame the batterer. Once they know the woman is safe and is agreeable to do this, they go out and publicly name her batterer." That serves a dual purpose. It makes the man "socially uncomfortable," and it raises cultural awareness of the problem.

As further evidence of progress, Marin notes that shelters for women now exist in Indonesia, the Philippines, India, and Japan. Battered women in Beijing can call a hot line, and the first shelter in Shanghai recently opened.

Changing Male Attitudes

Still, to prevent domestic violence from occurring at all, men's groups are working to change male attitudes.

Rob Gallup, executive director of Amend, a counseling program for abusive men in Denver, allows no "cultural excuse" for violence.

"Many of the Mexicans we treat tell us they can go back to Mexico and beat their wives with impunity," Mr. Gallup says. "I'm not sure if that's true. But whatever the culture, we just deal with it forthrightly. We tell them there is no excuse for domestic violence, and it's against the law."

Rather than accepting such behavior as macho, Gallup says, "We try to reframe it by saying, 'You're not macho if you beat your wife. You're less than a man. As an adult male, nobody can make you do anything. Nor do you have a cultural sanction to do it. You must control yourself—your actions, your thoughts. There's no way you can control another person. A whole man doesn't hit women. A whole man is able to respect his family.'"

Other counselors second that approach. As Cordero awaited a pretrial hearing on July 24, 1997, on charges of assault and battery, fans and sports columnists were joining a chorus criticizing him for what they regarded as a lack of contrition. [Cordero pled guilty on November 3, 1997; he was given a suspended sentence and required to complete a 40-week course for batterers.]

Making a case for this kind of public pressure and disapproval that encompass "the whole fabric of society," Nichols says, "It's not just the responsibility of legal or law enforcement groups. All institutions need to come out and say there is zero tolerance for abuse."

VIOLENCE IN TEENAGE RELATIONSHIPS

Christina Nifong

Christina Nifong reports that nearly one-third of teenage relationships involve some form of abuse. Peer pressure and inexperience in dating, she claims, contribute to the prevalence of dating violence among teenagers. The author describes a variety of approaches being used to help young women learn to speak up about the abuse they are experiencing. For example, in Massachusetts, schools have presented the play *The Yellow Dress*, which is about a young woman who was killed in an abusive relationship, Nifong writes. She also cites the importance of preventive programs that discuss the development of healthy relationships. Nifong is a staff writer for the *Christian Science Monitor*.

When counselors began teaching teens several years ago how to avoid future domestic violence, they had a rude awakening. They were too late.

Many of the high school students were already involved in abusive relationships, but they hadn't been coming forward out of confusion or fear. The outreach coordinators from battered women's programs quickly changed tactics, focusing on raising awareness and spurring research.

"We're in the schools and we're finding out that we don't have to wait," says Patricia Giggans, executive director of the Los Angeles Commission on Assaults Against Women.

At a time when the art of steering a child safely through adolescence means parents must be savvy about the signs of drug use and eating disorders, psychologists are raising another red flag: dating violence. Recent research shows that one-third of all teenage relationships include emotional, sexual, or physical abuse. Peer pressure, the media, and teen inexperience with dating are to blame, experts say.

Luz Troche can attest to the problem. Sitting in a cafeteria at Montachusett Regional Vocational Technical School in Fitchburg, Mass., the high school student explains that she has already struggled with an abusive boyfriend. "He was too possessive. I had to leave him."

The fact that teens are incorporating violence into their early relationships is hard for many adults—and especially parents—to believe, says Ms. Giggans, who is also co-author of *What Parents Need to Know About Dating Violence*.

"Folks are just beginning to start talking about this stuff," she says. "We don't teach our teens how to have good relationships. This is a big arena that's up for big discussion, and we're not having enough of it."

The impact of teen dating violence looms large for society. In addition to concerns about a victim's mental and physical well-being and the cost of rehabilitating or incarcerating abusers, a community loses a valuable future teacher or accountant or lawyer if the victim drops out of school. If an abused teen is pregnant, she is more likely to expose her child to violence, extending the chain of abuse.

"This has wide ramifications," says David Sugarman, a psychology professor at Rhode Island College in Providence.

Peer Pressure Is a Primary Factor

Peer pressure—so intense during adolescence—is one of the factors most to blame. Boys, who most often are the abusers, find others sanctioning violence. Aggressive behavior is rewarded on the playing field. Boys are seen as "macho" or "cool" to their male friends if they have a girlfriend and can control her, Professor Sugarman says.

For teenage girls, there is pressure to be in a relationship, regardless of how damaging it may be. Cutting ties to a popular boy can be extremely difficult, Sugarman says. A girl's friends may even reinforce the idea that it's okay for her boyfriend to hit her.

A teen's dating inexperience also contributes to unhealthy relationships. It can make a girl misread what older women would more easily identify as emotional or physical control. She may see her boyfriend's controlling behavior as normal, or even a sign of attentiveness.

"I think it's even harder for teens to get out of an abusive relationship [than adult women]," says Barri Rosenbluth, head of the Austin Teen Dating Violence Project at the Center for Battered Women in Austin, Texas. "They don't have anything to compare it to. What I see so often is that they're trying so hard to prove to their parents that they can be independent and they have good judgment."

Women are particularly susceptible during their teen years, when they stop thinking of their own growth. They start focusing on how to win boys' approval, says Joan Quinlan, project officer for Girl Power, a program of the US Department of Health and Human Services that seeks to prevent girls from becoming involved in drug use, crime, and sexual activity.

Between ages 9 and 14, girls are often encouraged, either by parents or peers, to stop the activities they once excelled in, such as sports or music, Ms. Quinlan says. Often they get the message that looks are what count.

"During that time period is when the confidence and pride that girls had when they were younger is either strengthened or weakened or becomes nonexistent," she says.

Addressing the Problem of Dating Violence

As awareness grows, women's shelters, district attorneys' offices, schools, and state legislatures have begun to focus on the problem of dating violence—though it still does not receive the attention that domestic violence, juvenile crime, or even date rape does.

Curricula are being developed for the nation's classrooms. Advocates are pushing for more evaluation of the programs in place. Scholars are researching the links between alcohol and drug abuse and dating violence.

One program offered in the Massachusetts schools is a play called *The Yellow Dress*, sponsored by a group founded after the death of a woman in her 20s who was in an abusive relationship.

The drama tells the tale of a young woman who is killed by her boyfriend after more than a year of his controlling her and sometimes beating her violently. After the play, students break into groups to discuss how they can avoid dating violence and help friends and family members understand the phenomenon.

Luz, who saw the performance at her school, says the story rang true to her. When you're in an abusive relationship, she comments, "you can't go out with your friends; he won't let you. He will grab you and shake you."

More comprehensive programs have also been developed to address teen-dating violence across the country.

The March of Dimes Prevention of Battery During Teen Pregnancy Project in the San Francisco Bay area focuses on violence against teens who are pregnant. Research shows that 1 in 5 pregnant teens is abused.

The March of Dimes has launched a public-information campaign, formed a coalition of government and service providers to keep pregnant teens from falling through the cracks, and opened one of the few teen shelters in the country that will take in a young woman and her child.

Pregnant teens who are abused often cannot go to shelters for teens or to those for battered women. The March of Dimes shelter, however, caters to pregnant teens' needs in its counseling groups, and offers such services as having program workers go to wherever a girl is staying and bring her to the shelter.

Programs That Promote Prevention

Promoting Alternatives to Violence Through Education (PAVE) in Denver is a center that helps youths ages 8 to 18. They have developed a preventive curriculum taught in many of the area schools. Additionally, they offer counseling for victims of teen dating violence and reha-

bilitation for abusing teens. The program also hosts a family enrich-
ment program that targets children who have witnessed domestic violence and offers them six free counseling sessions when their mother
applies for a restraining order against her boyfriend or husband.

Massachusetts has a unique program in which the state provides
grants to school districts willing to develop a teen-dating violence
prevention effort. The effort calls for schools to include the local
police department, battered women's shelters, and parents in their
planning. As of December 1996, 31 districts have signed on. Between
1994 and 1996, the grant has funded the training of teachers and
police officers and the adoption of teen-dating curricula in the
schools. The money allows schools to bring performances like *The Yellow Dress* to campus.

Players on all sides of the issue say these types of model programs
need to be duplicated so they can reach more teens. "Lately, there's
been a real recognition of the issue of teen-dating violence," says Pam
Ellis, of the Norfolk County, Mass., district attorney's office. "But I
still don't think it's enough."

Researchers also say they are now pointing their programming in a
new direction—less talk about single issues and more talk about how
to create healthy relationships in general.

"I like to call it the back-door approach," says Girl Power's Quinlan, "addressing developmental issues rather than hitting kids over
the head with a specific message or theme."

CHAPTER 2

HELP FOR VICTIMS OF ABUSE

THE POLICE RESPONSE

Albert R. Roberts

Albert R. Roberts is a professor of social work and criminal justice at Rutgers University Graduate School of Social Work in New Brunswick, New Jersey. In the following selection, taken from his book *Helping Battered Women: New Perspectives and Remedies*, Roberts examines the past, present, and future of police responses to domestic violence. In the past, he explains, domestic violence was considered a private matter, but in recent years police departments throughout the country have begun to implement laws and policies that require officers to protect battered women. Furthermore, he suggests that continued efforts to support specialized police training, community-wide intervention programs, and technological developments will help improve the ability of law enforcement personnel to protect battered women. Strengthening the police response to domestic violence, the author concludes, sends a message to violent abusers that society believes battering women is a serious crime.

It was 1400 hours on September 6, 2010. Two police officers were dispatched by headquarters on a report of a domestic violence complaint. Upon arriving at the scene, the officers spoke to the victim, Wilma R. She stated that her boyfriend, Louis, had been drinking the night before and became involved in an argument with her that ended with his punching her in the face and choking her. The officers observed that Wilma had a cut on her upper lip and swelling in the area between her nose and mouth.

When the police officers questioned Louis, he said he never touched her. He insisted that the bruises on her face resulted from her being clumsy and falling down the steps while carrying the laundry. He said she was making up the story of being beaten because she was angry at him for staying out late with his buddies the previous night.

Checking the Evidence

In order to determine whether or not Louis had choked his girlfriend, the police officer went to the car and brought in the compact portable laser unit. By aiming the laser at Wilma's neck, the officer immediately obtained laser fingerprints, which he compared with Louis's. The results showed an identical match. While the first officer was matching the fingerprints, the second officer went to the car and turned on the Mobile Digital Terminal (MDT) computer to run a computerized criminal history on Louis. In less than thirty seconds, Louis's history appeared on the screen: two prior convictions for simple assault against a former girlfriend and resisting arrest. The incidents had occurred three years earlier in another state. In addition, Louis's record showed two arrests during the past three years for driving while intoxicated.

The officers' next step was to obtain a temporary restraining order (TRO) to prevent Louis from having any further contact with Wilma. They obtained the TRO by entering a summary of their findings at the scene on their portable computer and using the cellular phone to call the judge to inform her that the report was being faxed to her courtroom from their car fax.

At the courthouse, the court clerk took the report from the fax machine and brought it to Judge Catherine Sloan for her signature. The court clerk then faxed the TRO back to the police car. The entire approval process took only fifteen minutes.

Next, the police transported Louis to the county jail, where the nurse practitioner implanted a subdural electronic sensor in Louis's wrist. The police also gave a sensing receiver to Wilma to wear externally, on a chain around her neck. The computer at police headquarters will monitor these sensors, as it has done with the 300 other domestic abuse cases reported to the police department during the past twelve months. The officers told Louis that if he came within a distance of 500 meters from Wilma, the sensing device would immediately alert the police officers that he had violated the TRO, and he would be sent to prison.

Police Response in the Mid-1990s

During the past few years, domestic violence has increasingly been defined as a serious crime (i.e., a felony rather than a misdemeanor) by a growing number of state criminal codes and family court statutes. In fact, because of the prevalence and life-threatening nature of woman battering, all fifty states have passed civil and/or criminal statutes to protect battered women. In some areas, as many as 75 percent of all police calls involve domestic conflict and/or violence. In the past, police were often reluctant to respond to family violence calls, and when they did respond, they were frequently accused of taking the side of the male batterers and subscribing to the view that "a man's home is his castle." Furthermore, the court staff tended to minimize the dangers that battered women encountered and discouraged them from filing criminal or civil complaints.

But now society at large has finally recognized that beating women (wives, cohabitants, or companions) is a crime and a major social problem. This recognition of woman abuse as a major social problem grew out of four noteworthy activities: (1) the women's movement, (2) two national prevalence studies on the extent of domestic violence in the United States, (3) books and news articles on battered women, and (4) recent litigation and legal reforms. Moreover, many police departments now have a proarrest or presumptive arrest policy. But the road toward implementing effective mandatory or proarrest policies for batterers has been bumpy and uneven, and research studies on the short-term deterrent effects of arresting batterers are inconclusive. Nevertheless, Americans have come a long way from the time when the use of violence by men to control their partners was condoned. Mandatory and warrantless arrest laws are just one part of the improved police response to victims of battering. In addition, the police in highly populated cities and counties throughout the nation now provide immediate protection to battered women. . . .

Although the recognition of domestic violence as a pervasive social problem is fairly recent, its cultural bases are deeply embedded in Western history and culture. Even a cursory review of that history reveals the extent to which law and society have traditionally served to implicitly support and perpetuate the subordination of women to their husbands. In some parts of Latin America and Asia, especially in the upper classes, killing a wife for an indiscretion has usually been acceptable, although the same privilege is not usually extended to women as perpetrators. Various cultures and societies have permitted or tacitly encouraged some degree of family violence as a means to maintain that subordination. Demographic analyses of domestic violence offenses reported to the police confirm the observation that domestic violence is most frequently perpetrated by males against their female partners, that males comprise only a small fraction of the total number of victims in domestic violence cases reported to the police. . . .

History reveals that until fairly recently, men were legally permitted to employ relatively unrestrained physical force against their wives and children in order to maintain family discipline. During the 1960s, several discrete trends evolved in policing, law, and politics that ultimately converged in the 1970s and 1980s to set the stage for our current concerns and the attention paid to domestic violence issues. The confluence of these trends and pressures created a unique and powerful synergy, forcing American police agencies and lawmakers to reexamine their policies and practices and to adopt the type of strategies that prevail today.

Specialized Police Training

Police recruit and in-service training provide an important part of teaching police their roles and responsibilities. The amount and duration of domestic violence training influence whether or not new police officers will take seriously their potential role in protecting battered women.

During the eight years from 1985 to 1993, a growing number of police departments incorporated training sessions on family violence into their police academy curricula. These specialized training sessions have been implemented much more frequently in large city or county police training academies than in small towns. In addition, many police departments now require all officers to arrest a domestic violence suspect when the victim exhibits signs of bodily injury, when a weapon is involved in the commission of a domestic violence act, or when there is probable cause to believe that the named accuser has violated the terms of a restraining order or other no-contact court order.

The author conducted a national survey on domestic violence training and police responses to battered women. The survey was sent to sixty police chiefs and their staff in metropolitan areas in every region of the United States. The study's findings indicated a wide variation in the amount of time devoted to specialized domestic violence training for new recruits, ranging from a total of three hours to forty hours at the police academies located in the largest cities, such as Baltimore, Boston, Indianapolis, Kansas City, Las Vegas, Memphis, Milwaukee, San Diego, Seattle, and Tucson. Most small-town police departments provide no training on domestic violence or victim rights. In these smaller towns and municipalities, state police or troopers are called in to intervene in domestic violence cases.

Training State Police

State troopers are responsible for protecting residents in many rural areas that have no local police department or when the nearest law enforcement agency is the county sheriff's office. The majority of state police are trained to respond in a sensitive and compassionate way to battered women. In general, state police academies provide comprehensive training to all state troopers on such policies and procedures, changes in the state criminal code, motor vehicle violations, investigative techniques, victims' rights legislation, and domestic violence.

Beginning in fiscal year 1991, the federal Office for Victims of Crime of the U.S. Department of Justice began funding and providing technical assistance to state police training academies. The purpose of these federal grants has been to develop and implement training programs for state and county law enforcement administrators and officers on the current policies and procedures for responding to family violence incidents. Each year a different group of eight to ten states receives a two-year federal training grant to develop family violence training courses and related materials. . . .

Proarrest Policies

Since 1984, the trend has been for a growing number of police departments in cities with a population of more than 100,000 to adopt a
policy of proarrest or probable-cause arrests of batterers. Efforts to
redefine battering as a crime were boosted significantly by the following four activities and studies:

1. The National Coalition Against Domestic Violence as well as
   statewide coalitions and advocacy groups are working to protect
   battered women.
2. The Minneapolis domestic violence experiment on the deterrent
   effects of arrest.
3. The final report of the U.S. Attorney General's Task Force on
   Family Violence, citing the Minneapolis experiment, documenting the prevalence and intense dangers of battering episodes,
   and concluding that domestic violence is a major crime problem
   and that criminal justice agencies should handle it as such.
4. Television network and newspaper accounts of the court decisions that held police liable for failing to protect battered
   women from severe injuries.

A highly publicized Supreme Court case in the mid-1980s led to
proarrest laws and mandated police training on intervening in domestic violence incidents. In this case, Tracey Thurman of Torrington,
Connecticut, who had been beaten repeatedly by her husband, sued
the Torrington police department. The basis for her lawsuit was the
failure of the police department to protect her, even though she had
continually requested police protection over an eight-month period.
And even though Ms. Thurman had obtained a court order barring
her violent spouse from assaulting her again, it took the police twenty-five minutes to arrive on the scene of the most violent battering.
After arriving at the Thurman home, the arresting officer delayed
arresting Mr. Thurman for several minutes, giving him, who had a
bloody knife in hand, plenty of time to repeatedly kick his wife in the
head, face, and neck while she lay helpless on the ground. As a result,
Ms. Thurman suffered life-threatening injuries, including multiple
stab wounds to the chest, neck, and face; fractured cervical vertebrae
and damage to her spinal cord; partial paralysis below the neck; lacer-
ations to the cheeks and mouth; loss of blood; shock; scarring; severe
pain; and mental anguish. Tracey Thurman's award was unprecedent-
ed: $2.3 million in compensatory damages against twenty-four police
officers. The jury found that the Torrington, Connecticut, police had
deprived Ms. Thurman of her constitutional right to equal protection
under the law (Fourteenth Amendment of the Constitution). The jury
further concluded that the Torrington police officers were guilty of
gross negligence in failing to protect Tracey Thurman and her son
Charles, Jr., from the violent acts of Charles Thurman, Sr.

The Police Respond to Changing Laws

In the wake of the court decision in the Thurman case, police departments throughout the country began implementing proarrest policies and increased police training on domestic violence. Therefore, during the latter half of the 1980s and the first half of the 1990s, there was a proliferation of police training courses on how best to handle domestic violence calls.

By 1988, ten states had passed laws expanding the police's arrest powers in cases of domestic assault. Specifically, these new statutes require arrest when there is a positive determination of probable cause (i.e., the existence of a visible injury and/or the passage of only a small amount of time between the commission of the assault and the arrival of the police). Police departments are also legally required to arrest batterers who have violated protective or restraining orders granted to battered women by the courts. As of 1992, protective orders were available to abused women in fifty states and the District of Columbia. In more and more jurisdictions, women in abusive relationships have obtained a protective order against their abuser from their local court in order to prevent him from coming to their residence. Police are called upon to enforce the protective order and to arrest the abuser if he violates any stipulations in the court order.

Several issues, however, limit the effectiveness of proarrest policies. First, in many jurisdictions, unmarried couples are not included in the proarrest policy for domestic violence. This certainly limits the police, since it is generally recognized that the police receive proportionately more domestic violence calls from cohabiting women than from married women. Second, several studies have indicated that 40 to 60 percent of batterers flee the residence before the police arrive on the scene. Therefore, the batterer would not be arrested unless the battered victim signed a criminal complaint. The final issue relates to the fact that experienced police officers are used to making their own decisions regarding whether or not to arrest an abusive person. As a result, police compliance with a presumptive or proarrest domestic violence policy will be a gradual process, taking several years.

Despite all the limitations inherent in instituting a proarrest policy, considerable progress has been made in the past decade. Although the arrest of all suspects in domestic violence calls is mandatory in only a small number of states, thousands of police departments nationwide are now making arrests when the officer observes signs of bodily injury on the battered woman.

Technological Protection for Victims

Technology is beginning to protect battered women from their abusive partners. It is also deterring some violent batterers from repeating their abusive and brutal acts. Recent developments in electronic mon-

itors, computerized tracking of offenders and victims, and video sur-
veillance have greatly bolstered crime investigations and crime prevention efforts. The goal is to lessen and eventually eliminate violent
crime by controlling the physical environment. In most severe cases,
the formerly battered woman agrees to maintain an active restraining
order, agrees to testify in court and cooperate with any criminal proceedings against the alleged batterer, has a telephone in her residence,
and believes that she is in extreme danger of aggravated assault or
attempted murder by the defendant. In these cases, a home electronic
monitor (e.g., panic alarm or pendant), also known as the abused
woman's active emergency response pendant, can deter the batterer
from violating his restraining order.

Private security companies recently began donating and marketing
electronic security devices called panic alarms to battered women.
The main purpose of these portable alarms, which have a range of
about 200 feet from the victim's home, is to provide the battered
women with an immediate and direct link to their local police in an
emergency with just a press of a button. In some jurisdictions in Colorado and New Hampshire, the electronic pendant alarms are coupled
with electronic monitoring of batterers through the Juris Monitor
ankle bracelet, manufactured by B.I., Inc. If the batterer comes within
close proximity of the victim's home, the ankle bracelet sounds a loud
alarm in the home and immediately alerts the police. ADT Security
has set up electronic pendants for battered women in thirty counties
and cities throughout the United States. The women are carefully
selected for each program by a screening committee comprised of
community leaders including a prosecutor or deputy prosecutor, a
supervisor from the local battered women's shelter, and a police
administrator. In all cases, the victim has an active restraining order
against the batterer and is willing to fully cooperate with the prosecutor's office. One major drawback of these alarms is that the unit will
not work if the telephone line is cut or not working.

Several companies—including T.L.P. Technologies, Inc.; Transcience;
and B.I. Inc.—are currently developing electronic monitors. The alarm
system developed by T.L.P. Technologies works even when the phone
lines are down and when there is no electrical power. In the victim's
home, police install the system, which includes a radio transmitter
with a battery backup, an antenna, and a remote panic or motion-
detector device. T.L.P.'s Visibility Plus Radio Data Alarm System inte-
grates both the alarm system and computer-generated data immediately into the police radio channel instead of using a private security
company as an intermediary. This system has been used with hundreds
of battered women in both Nassau and Suffolk Counties, New York.

The most promising device that pinpoints the location of the victim whether she is at home, at work, or in the supermarket was developed by Geo Satellite Positioning Equipment. This advanced technol-

ogy works by means of a satellite that sends a special signal from a receiver on the ground to the local police computer screen. A street map comes on the screen and sends a burst of data over the network, including the alarm number and the longitude and latitude of the victim's location within 5 to 10 feet.

Because of the growing awareness of the acute injuries sustained by battered women throughout the United States, and the millions of dollars spent on health and mental health care for victims of domestic violence, I predict that the electronic-monitoring programs will be expanded to thousands of battered women in every state by the year 2010. Unfortunately, as has been the case with other new legislation, a "high-profile" crisis situation needs to occur before Congress enacts new legislation.

Both short-term emergency support and long-term security services are critically needed by battered women and their children. It seems important that emergency services, including electronic pendants, be initiated for the thousands of battered women in imminent danger of suffering repeated assaults and being murdered by their former abusive partners. Funding for the new technology should come from both corporate sponsors and government agencies. But first, research needs to be carried out to determine which emergency electronic systems are most effective in protecting battered women. Also, under what conditions does the electronic technology fail to ensure the battered women's safety? *Before new electronic technology is purchased by battered women's shelters and law enforcement agencies, it is critical that comprehensive evaluations and outcome studies be planned and carried out.*

Community-Wide Intervention Programs

Some populated cities and communities have developed citywide and community-wide task forces in order to provide a well-coordinated response to domestic family violence from the police, the courts, victim/witness assistance, and social service agencies. Many of these community task forces have followed the model of the programs developed during the 1980s in such areas as Baltimore County, Maryland; Quincy, Massachusetts; Duluth and Minneapolis, Minnesota; Boulder and Denver, Colorado; Memphis, Tennessee; Milwaukee, Wisconsin; Lincoln, Nebraska; and Seattle, Washington. For coordination to be effective among battered women's shelters, police, prosecutors, victim/witness assistance programs, and batterers' counseling programs, certain policies and practices are required. For example, shelter directors should offer to speak at police roll calls and police training sessions. These program directors have an important role in educating the police command and line personnel about the vital role of police in arresting and taking the batterers into custody and transporting battered women to the hospital emergency room and/or shelter. Police chiefs should define domestic violence as a serious crime; be willing to instill this view in their captains, lieutenants, sergeants, and patrol officers; and adopt mandatory arrest policies and implement a systematic monitoring program to check compliance with these new policies. Police commissioners and chiefs should also require all officers to complete training on the myths of domestic violence, the psychosocial characteristics of battered women and their abusers, the situations in which it is appropriate to wake a magistrate in the middle of the night to obtain a temporary restraining order for the victim, and why more arrests of batterers are needed. In addition, it is critical that police chiefs work closely with prosecutors and judges to make sure that arrest policies are supported by prosecutions and sanctions in the form of fines, jail time, and/or deferred prosecution pending the outcome of six months of court-mandated batterers counseling.

Sending a Message to Society

Mandatory arrest and eight to twelve hours in jail to cool off are certainly not a panacea to domestic violence. Although substantial progress has been made in strengthening domestic violence laws and improving police training, much remains to be done. Even if arresting them helps deter otherwise law-abiding abusive partners and even if arrest deters only a small percentage of abusers, it is still much more humane than doing nothing. That is, arresting the violent abuser conveys the important message to abusive adults, children, and society at large that family violence is a serious crime. But if the police refuse to arrest the batterer, they are conveying the message that family violence is tolerated and acceptable.

Warrentless arrest by law enforcement officers is one primary part of society's improved response to victims of battering. Responsive communities must work toward an integrated response from the police, the courts, and social service agencies. Victims of domestic violence often have multiple legal, psychological, and social service needs. Therefore, a well-coordinated community-wide approach by all mental health, social service, judicial, and law enforcement agencies should be planned and implemented throughout the United States.

UNIVERSAL SCREENING FOR A UNIVERSAL PROBLEM

Linda Poirier

In the following selection, Linda Poirier explores the importance of universal screening for domestic violence. Poirier asserts that many women from higher socioeconomic backgrounds are not screened for domestic violence because they do not fit the profile of battered women who use shelters and public service agencies. She argues that battered women from higher socioeconomic groups are more likely to appear at primary care and family therapy practices, which do not often screen for domestic violence even though it occurs at higher rates than many other health care problems. Pointing out that domestic violence meets the U.S. Public Health Service's guidelines for universal screening, Poirier maintains that establishing a system of routine screening would help identify and protect abused women from all socioeconomic groups. Poirier is a nurse practitioner at Eau Claire Women's Care in Eau Claire, Wisconsin.

Our nation has been captured since 1994 by three high-profile cases involving domestic violence: a nationally televised court trial involving domestic violence, an admission of another famous sports figure that he had physically abused his wife, and a resignation of a public official after he was charged with abusing his wife. Public awareness and research efforts aimed at disclosing the secret of domestic violence began in the 1970s as part of the broader feminist agenda. The difference between the 1970s public depiction of domestic violence and the more recently published picture is that these women, whose lives were made public after their partners were charged with domestic violence, all had adequate financial resources, access to health care, educational advantages, and adequate housing. Why did they stay? Why didn't they get help? How did they fall through the cracks?

Public service messages boom the following statement: "Every 15 seconds a woman is physically abused by her husband or lover." Domestic violence is not, and never has been, a "disease" of the poor.

Adapted, with permission, from Linda Poirier, "The Importance of Screening for Domestic Violence in All Women," *The Nurse Practitioner*, vol. 22, no. 5, pp. 105–22, © Springhouse Corporation, Springhouse, Pa.

Thousands of women from high socioeconomic levels are beginning to shatter our visual image of an abused woman and are forcing us to look at current primary care screening practices and interventions. The purpose of this article is to provide a rationale for the universal screening of all women for domestic abuse, including women who appear "picture perfect."

Domestic violence has been defined by W.J. Listwan as "a pattern of coercive control and terror that one person uses over another." This control may or may not involve actual physical injury and includes psychological (verbal assaults and criticisms) and economic abuse (the creation of financial dependence). Adult members of a family are most often the victims and perpetrators of abuse, although the violence can extend to children and elders. According to V.P. Tilden and P. Shepherd, children who witness or who are victims of domestic violence can eventually come to view this violent behavior as a "learned phenomenon," and thus the behavior is often transmitted from generation to generation.

The Cost of Domestic Violence

Family violence is seen as a growing national problem that carries with it many health care implications. The monetary cost of domestic violence involves costly emergency room visits, repeated clinic visits, time lost from work due to injuries, hospitalizations, mental health counseling, and the cost of maintaining domestic violence services within the community. Far greater are the emotional and psychologic costs of family violence. Victims of domestic violence often suffer from depression and other emotional injuries related to the persistent degradation of their self-esteem and psychologic functioning as a result of the abuse. Both the current and past Surgeon Generals of the United States and the Public Health objectives for Healthy People 2000 have identified family violence as an epidemic and have called for an organized approach to screen, treat, and prevent further violence.

The literature is replete with statistics regarding the incidence of domestic violence. It is estimated that patterns of domestic abuse are repeated in the lives of 2 million to 4 million Americans annually. Domestic violence leads to 28,700 emergency room visits per year, 39,000 physician office visits, $44 million in total annual medical costs, and 175,000 lost days of work. More disturbing yet is the report that more than half of the women murdered in the United States are killed by their male partners. Most of these statistics were gathered from social service agencies and battered women shelters and may not be reflective of women who seek help privately and are of greater means. A current literature review reveals only one study whose sample consisted of middle-class women who had sought routine care at a military hospital. In this study there was an overall 21% prevalence rate of physical abuse occurring mainly among younger women who worked outside the home. It has also been speculated that because of the secretive nature of domestic violence, underreporting of its incidence is likely, and in fact, the U.S. Department of Justice (1980) estimates that 43% of spousal abuse incidents are not reported to the police.

The Profile of a Battered Woman

The majority of articles that address domestic violence include a statement about its permeability across all socioeconomic levels, but the victim profiles that describe the battered woman and subsequent interventions may not reflect the reality of women in higher socioeconomic groups. Research with battered women has focused on identifying characteristics of the battered woman to help health care practitioners working in primary care settings and mental health agencies identify and intervene with these women. Most of these projects were carried out in shelters and public service agencies. The subsequent typical profile of a battered woman is depicted in Table 1.

Table 1. Profile of Battered Women Who Use Shelters and Public Service Agencies

1. Socially isolated and withdrawn
2. Feels trapped in marriage/relationship
3. Has poor impulse control
4. Has low self-esteem
5. May have been abused or witnessed abuse as a child
6. May feel abuse is her fault
7. May be depressed and/or suicidal
8. Is usually financially dependent on spouse
9. May abuse drugs and alcohol
10. May be apathetic
11. Has a trusting nature
12. Is nonaggressive and traditional

Although this profile may reflect the characteristics of women who utilize shelters and social services, it may not accurately reflect a large segment of women in higher socioeconomic groups who may choose not to seek help at shelters. This stereotype, or set of common denominators, may also put the blame for the abuse on the victim; a position that must be carefully avoided. More recent research has found that there is not a set of common denominators between women who are abused or their abusers.

In a study consisting of 6,000 women who sought help from shelters in Texas, the profile of the passive, weak woman who does not seek help was dispelled. E.W. Gondolf contends that for many years, researchers have believed that battered women suffer from "learned helplessness." The concept of learned helplessness is based on the premise that if a person experiences repeated incongruences between responses and outcomes to situations, they will give up and accept situations as they occur. Gondolf's study replaces the concept of learned helplessness with a theory of survivorship. This new theory is based on observations that many women in abusive situations have been found to actively seek help and creatively survive in abusive situations. The theory of survivorship is not consistent with society's previous perspective of domestic abuse. Thus, screening for domestic violence becomes difficult, and the perpetuation of the stereotypical battered woman prevents us from viewing the universality of this problem.

Battered Women of Higher Socioeconomic Status

Women of higher socioeconomic status may display some of these same characteristics, but they may manifest these characteristics differently. They may experience social isolation related to repeated geographical moves associated with the corporate mobility of the 1990s. They may present themselves in public as being self-assured and assertive, yet at home may be passive and apathetic, believing they are the root of their family's dysfunction. They may drive a Mercedes Benz but be unable to write a check without their husband's approval, thereby maintaining their financial dependence. They may present themselves as the perfect wife and mother to all the other families at the health club, but behind the well-rehearsed facade be living a life of terror and humiliation.

Detection of abuse within primary care settings and family therapy practices has historically been low. In a survey administered to marriage and family therapists, 60% of the respondents did not identify family violence as a significant problem in their practice. This is despite other research that indicates that up to 70% of clients in family therapy have been victims of family violence. In another study of primary care physicians, as few as 1 in 20 battered women were correctly diagnosed by their physician. In 1992, L.K. Hamberger reported that only 6 of 364 women surveyed who had sought care were asked about abuse by their health care provider.

Women who are battered often present to their primary care providers with frequent somatic complaints. These complaints range from insomnia, depression, irritability, and suicidal ideation to abdominal pain, pelvic pain, chest pain, and headaches. Unfortunately, these help-seeking efforts go largely unmet when women are not routinely and universally screened for domestic violence. The opportunities for assessment and intervention are being provided by these women as they seek health care. Primary health care practitioners need to seize the moment. In 1992, K.J. Fullin provided the following battered woman's testimony:

> I was terrified that someone would ask me how I got my injuries. I was just as terrified that no one would ask and I

would have to return home without talking to anyone about
what was happening to me.

Routine Screening of Health Care Problems

Routine screening for conditions that occur at rates equal to or less
than domestic violence have become standard. As M.R. Sassetti states:

> Although correctly diagnosing this health care problem
> (domestic violence) is the exception, screening for it is nearly
> nonexistent. This entity is at least as common as breast can-
> cer and far more common than thyroid problems, hyperten-
> sion, and colon cancer, for which primary care physicians
> routinely screen. In pregnant populations, battering occurs at
> a frequency far greater than the incidence of rubella, Rh and
> ABO incompatibilities, hepatitis, and diabetes combined, yet
> unlike these frequently occurring maladies, it is rarely, if ever,
> screened for, let alone appropriately diagnosed in the 1 in 10
> to 1 in 4 obstetric patients who are battered.

The U.S. Public Health Service's Put Prevention into Practice campaign utilizes the following guidelines in determining when a screening test is useful:
1. The condition must have a significant effect on the quality and
   quantity of life.
2. Acceptable methods of treatment must be available.
3. The condition must have an asymptomatic period during which
   detection and treatment significantly reduce morbidity or mor-
   tality.
4. Treatment in the asymptomatic phase must yield a therapeutic
   result superior to that obtained by delaying treatment until
   symptoms appear.
5. Tests that are acceptable to patients must be available, at a reasonable cost, to detect the condition in the asymptomatic period.
6. The incidence of the condition must be sufficient to justify the
   cost of the screening.

Screening for domestic violence clearly meets these requirements.
Living in an abusive environment significantly decreases a person's
quality of life and can lead to premature death. Since the 1970s there
has been a concerted effort by state agencies and grassroots coalitions
to meet the needs of abused women. Although changes in funding are
creating concern, most communities have resources available to
women in varying degrees of comprehensiveness. If the quality of
exchange within personal relationships is assessed during patient/ practitioner encounter, the characteristic patterns of abuse may be detected
before any abuse occurs. If domestic abuse patterns can be detected and
treatment instituted before an assault, the woman's self-esteem, personal locus of control, safety, and possibly marriage can be saved. Self-

report and interview questionnaires are available and inexpensive to administer. The incidence of domestic violence far exceeds that of other diseases commonly screened for in the primary care setting.

Screening Procedures for Domestic Violence

For screening procedures to be effective, women need to be screened for domestic violence at every health maintenance visit and most interval visits to their primary care provider; especially if they repeatedly return with somatic complaints that go unresolved. As health care providers living in an age of rapid HIV transmission, we have had to become comfortable screening all women for unsafe sexual practices. Screening for domestic violence, if done routinely, will also attain a level of comfort as well as give patients the message that their health care provider cares about them and their health and safety.

In recent years there has been an increase in the number of tools available to screen for domestic violence. The Nursing Research Consortium of Violence and Abuse has developed a self-report pictorial screening tool that has been widely used by state and private providers caring for pregnant women. This tool could easily be adapted for use with all women.

In a study conducted by J. McFarlane, it was established that women had higher rates of abuse disclosure during a nurse interview (29.3%) than they did with a self-report tool (7.3%). This may be due to a host of factors: embarrassment, shame, fear of tool being seen by office personnel other than caregiver, and denial. This fear of disclosure can be reduced if the caregiver is trusted and apt to respond in a positive, nonjudgmental way. The embarrassment and shame may be even more significant for women from the same social milieu as the health care providers themselves. Women will increase the rate of disclosure if they are interviewed alone and with the knowledge that what they disclose will be kept confidential. . . .

Acting on the Results of Screening

If a patient screens negative, she should still be educated about the cycle of violence and how to protect herself from a potentially dangerous situation. The cycle of violence often follows a well-recognized pattern of tension-building within the relationship, a violent explosion, and a honeymoon phase. The tension-building phase is characterized by the relentless emotional battering and its subsequent destruction of the women's sense of self-worth and self-determination. When the tension reaches its peak, there is an explosion of violence and the tension is defused. The couple then enters the honeymoon phase that is typically characterized by the batterer profusely apologizing and pleading for forgiveness. Unfortunately, as time passes, the tension begins to build again, and the cycle repeats itself. Women need to be aware of this cycle and also the subtle ways that their partners may impose their control over them.

If a patient screens positive for domestic violence, it is important to stress that she is not to blame herself or to take responsibility for the abuse. Next, a more thorough assessment of the type, amount, severity, and duration of the abuse must be done as well as an assessment of her children's safety. She may need assistance to accurately assess the amount of danger she is currently experiencing. J.C. Campbell has developed a danger assessment tool to help victims and practitioners determine the level of risk present in the patient's living situation. The woman also needs to be informed of her legal rights and appropriate avenues of legal protection available to her within her community. Public disclosure may be especially difficult for the woman from a higher socioeconomic population. Her partner may be very visible within the community, and she may fear that the costs of social repercussions far outweigh the safety and respect she seeks.

Before the woman leaves the primary care facility, she needs to have information that will enable her to act when she is prepared to do so. This may simply be the number of the local shelter where she can obtain confidential counseling. Women of greater means may feel more comfortable obtaining counseling from a private therapist who is knowledgeable and experienced in helping battered women regain their sense of self-worth and self-respect to enable them to leave their abusive situation. Brochures describing local community resources for battered women can be discreetly placed in bathroom stalls enabling women to obtain the information privately.

A Message to Health Care Providers

Future research regarding domestic violence needs to better define the diverse backgrounds and experiences of battered women. Past research has focused on women from lower socioeconomic groups and has provided us with comprehensive abuse programs and services in most communities. Unfortunately, there is a silent and growing number of women from higher socioeconomic groups whose needs are not being met because current screening methods and services target the profile of the battered woman developed in the 1970s. Nurses, physicians, social workers, and others who are currently working with abuse victims from higher socioeconomic backgrounds can provide much needed clinical experience and observations to researchers. Sharing this valuable information can facilitate the publication of successful interventions enhancing current community programs and services.

Health care providers who routinely see women who are battered need to avoid succumbing to the "learned helplessness" syndrome themselves. A typical battered woman may leave and then return to her batterer as many as eight times before leaving permanently. This pattern of negative outcomes after interventions provided by the health care provider can lead to a sense of hopelessness on the part of the providers themselves. No one can predict when that eighth time will occur. Positive, empowering interventions can help women move one step closer to improving their lives and the lives of their children.

Domestic abuse extends into all neighborhoods and is occurring in epidemic numbers. Clinicians should implement universal screening and educating of all women, not just those who present with symptoms of abuse or fill the stereotypical picture of an abused woman. Primary care providers can increase the detection of potential and ongoing abuse and intervene before the patient becomes just another statistic.

COUNSELING THE VICTIM WHO HAS KILLED HER ABUSER

Evelyn J. Hall

The following selection is excerpted from the book *I Am Not Your Victim: Anatomy of Domestic Violence*, coauthored by Beth Sipe and Evelyn J. Hall. Sipe is a formerly battered woman who faced murder charges after she killed her husband Steven (Sam) Sipe on April 9, 1988; the charges were dismissed when the judge ruled that she had acted in self-defense. Hall, who wrote the section of the book from which this selection was taken, is a marriage and family therapist who counseled Sipe for seven years, beginning shortly after she killed her husband. From this experience, Hall provides guidelines for the counseling of battered women who have killed their abusers. Because these women mistrust the system and the professionals who failed to protect them from abuse, Hall argues, they are often fatalistic about the future and expect to be imprisoned. She recommends that counselors provide these women with support and validation in order to help them make positive decisions about their future.

Counseling a battered woman who has killed her abuser requires attention to the same principles outlined in 1987 by S. Schechter for counseling any battered woman. The focus is on empowering the woman through safety planning, validation of her experiences, exploration of her strengths, and respect for her right to self-determination. It means listening to her with compassion and acceptance, but without judging, blaming, or telling her what to do. As Beth Sipe's story illustrates, adherence to these principles is important, even if the woman begins treatment with the idea that it is too late for her to get help. The following sections will elaborate on these concepts.

An Immediate Focus on Safety
A battered woman who has killed her partner continues to need safety planning. The counselor cannot assume that danger of physical harm to the woman ended with the abuser's death. He may have fam-

ily or friends who threaten or attempt to harm her. Beth, for example, was harassed by callers who hung up after she answered and by threatening phone calls, prowlers, vandalism of her home and car, and gunfire in her backyard. Repeated unexpected appearances by the police at her home added to Beth's perception of imminent danger.

When the woman's safety continues to be threatened, safety options, such as an avenue of escape, shelter, safe storage and copying of important documents, and emergency phone numbers, should be discussed with her. Consideration of possible positive and negative consequences of each option should be part of this discussion. Rehearsal of her ultimate plan is helpful, and knowing what choices she can make in regard to safety also accesses her personal power.

Listening with compassion and acceptance to a battered woman's story is particularly important after she has killed her abuser. By the time death has occurred in a violent relationship, a woman has usually had many encounters with social services, mental health providers, and the justice system. Typically, these experiences have ranged from disappointing to disastrous, limiting her willingness to trust a new authority figure. This was certainly true in Beth's case. She had appealed unsuccessfully for help and protection many times throughout seventeen years of intense abuse.

Acceptance and Validation Are Important

At first, the woman may view the counselor as part of the establishment which has been nonresponsive. Consequently, the counselor's ability to maintain a nonjudgmental attitude is more critical than ever. Because the system has not responded to her cries for help, the woman may have concluded that no one cares about her safety. After she has killed her partner, she may give up hope of any future. In Beth's words during her first counseling session with me, "I don't know what I'm doing here. It's too late for me." For someone to listen to and accept her story gives her validation and may trigger some hope.

Another reason that acceptance is so important at this stage is the woman's emotional condition. As pointed out by A. Browne and L.E. Walker, a battered woman usually kills only in self-defense after prolonged severe abuse; she usually has no intent to kill. Understandably, her symptoms of posttraumatic stress disorder (PTSD) are extremely severe after her abuser's death. Mixed with PTSD symptoms are her grief and remorse about his death and how he died. Like Beth, the woman is likely to be shut down, exhibiting flat affect [little or no emotion], disorganized thought, disassociation, even indifference to helping herself. She may experience appetite disturbance, sleep disorder, and panic attacks that affect her physical health or become life threatening. She may view and label herself as "crazy." At some point, her anger about the years of abuse and about feeling forced to kill in self-defense will surface with a force that may frighten her. Like Beth, she may have sought counseling because someone else suggested or ordered that she do so.

The counselor—through nonjudgmental listening—offers her needed validation that she does matter and that her reaction is normal, not crazy. The counselor's role is to assist the woman in working through the maze of emotions in a safe, nurturing environment. Frequently, these emotions may surface in dreams, so the counselor should be prepared to do dream work or direct the client to a qualified professional who can.

Typically, a battered woman who remains in a violent relationship for a long period of time is viewed as weak-willed, masochistic, lacking intelligence, or all three. In fact, the opposite is true. She could not survive the years of abuse if she did not have great strength and resourcefulness. The counselor needs to assist her in identifying and exploring all her strengths. This task ultimately helps the woman reclaim her identity and self-esteem. Beth, for example, had demonstrated skill and persistence in her pursuit of education and medical training, as well as in her determination to earn money at any honest labor. Throughout the years of abuse, she was able to maintain relationships with her family and a few friends, so she usually had some support system. She was also a creative homemaker and devoted mother, budgeting limited monies and resources to ensure that her family always had the necessities of life.

Helping her to identify all her accomplishments was a critical step in her treatment. As she began to see herself as a person with strength and ability, she became increasingly motivated to handle daily tasks and problems, such as her job and her children. She also redoubled her efforts in her own defense.

Overall, Beth's level of functioning before the shooting was very high. In spite of extreme duress from her husband, Sam, she was able to maintain a full-time job as a medical aide, take on a part-time job as a movie extra, meet the demands of the court to get a larger apartment, and support herself and her children. Only in interactions with her husband did she exhibit signs of learned helplessness; she could excel in most other areas of her life. Thus, Beth clearly demonstrates that learned helplessness can be situational and limited to a battered woman's intimate relationship. For the counselor, recognition of this factor can help him or her maintain appropriate respect for the woman and her right to self-determination. The counselor should offer the woman maximum encouragement with minimal interference in her decisions.

Reconstructing the History of Abuse

Taking a complete history of the abuse experienced by a battered woman who has killed serves several therapeutic functions. It allows her to express her feelings about the abuse in safety, perhaps for the first time. Writing out this history is usually suggested as a means of confronting the reality of the abuse. Without a visible written history, the abuse remains shadowy, disjointed fragments in the woman's mind.

For a woman like Beth with so many years of abuse, addressing her history of abuse is a very emotional and lengthy process. It requires that the counselor balance therapeutic boundaries and structure with enough flexibility to respond to emergencies that inevitably arise while bringing such painful memories to the surface. There is a danger that the counselor can become so immersed in the woman's intense drama as to lose objectivity. Regular consultation with knowledgeable colleagues is not only helpful but also necessary for the counselor to maintain an objective perspective.

Through examination of her history of abuse, the woman may gradually complete expressions of feelings long buried and break free of her confusion about the relationship.

The counselor's role is to provide a safe, supportive environment and information about domestic violence as it is relevant. The cycle of violence, power and control tactics, characteristics of a batterer, and symptoms of PTSD are representative of subjects that almost always need explanations. The value of offering such information is evident in one of Beth's responses; that is, "Do these men go to abuse school?" Until she had access to this information, Beth thought she was a rare case. The information helped alleviate her feeling of shame about being abused and lessened the need for secrecy.

Why Did She Stay?

As instances of past abuse are processed, the woman begins to ask herself why she returned after separations and why she stayed in the relationship so long. These are questions Beth asked herself repeatedly. The counselor should allow the woman to identify her own reasons and validate those reasons through acceptance. The counselor can provide further validation by providing lists of reasons other battered women have given for staying or by suggesting written materials, such as O.W. Barnett and A.D. LaViolette's book on battered women leaving relationships.

Beth's primary reason for staying during the first ten years of her marriage coincides with the most frequent reason given by other battered women—love of the man. Although many people find this reason implausible, Walker points out that most people grew up in homes where physical punishment was linked to love. So physical violence in an adult relationship does not necessarily seem inconsistent with love to a battered woman or to the batterer. Exploration of different definitions of love may be helpful at this point, along with pinpointing what the woman expected going into the relationship. Conclusions she reaches about love and relationships may help her protect herself in the future. It may also help her come to peace with another recurrent question: How could he love me and treat me so badly?

It is the counselor's role to raise questions, suggest options, and offer support for the woman, whatever she concludes.

Reviewing a battered woman's history of abuse usually reveals ineffective responses by various professionals to her attempts to get help. In Beth's case, there were numerous such ineffective responses. Examination of these responses provides strong reasons to stop victim blaming, as well as indicators for effective intervention.

In 1973, Beth sought professional help through counseling. At that time, little had been written about treatment for domestic violence. Both counselors the couple saw offered practical suggestions to reduce conflicts, but they did not address Sam's violent and alcoholic behaviors. This gave Beth some validation, but it allowed Sam to dismiss the counselors as "outsiders" and "just a bunch of bull." Today, the recommended procedure is to screen all couples for violence during the initial phone call. If violence is present, knowledgeable counselors do not see the couple together until the man has completed his own therapy to eliminate the violence. The practice of seeing a violent couple together encourages the abuser to blame the woman for his behavior and often increases the danger to the woman, as shown by the Sipe case.

Individual counseling, either with a mental health professional or with clergy, is another way a battered woman often tries to get help. Initially, her purpose is "to get him to stop hurting me." If she continues in counseling, she may rebuild her self-esteem and regain her identity.

This was true for Beth with the psychologist and the pastor she saw during her years in Colorado. However, it should be noted that the improvement of her mental health did nothing to retard or end Sam's violence. On the contrary, Sam's violence escalated as he tried to maintain control over Beth. Counselors who see a battered woman individually must constantly caution the woman that changes in her behavior, for example, assertiveness, may increase the danger of intensified attacks by the batterer.

Sending a Message that Battering Is Acceptable

The battered woman who kills her abuser has—in most cases—made frequent calls to police agencies for help. Beth, for example, called police for help more times than can be counted, starting with calls to Blytheville, Arkansas, police in 1975. . . . Throughout the years of abuse, she continued to appeal to the police for help, but Sam was never given an appropriate consequence, such as mandatory counseling in a batterers' treatment program or jail time. This lack of consequences gives the man a clear message that his treatment of his partner is acceptable; it reinforces his battering behavior. Even when the Sipes lived in states (Colorado and Nevada) where mandatory arrest laws had been enacted, the police arrested him only twice. In those cases, the court did not apply an appropriate consequence, thereby increasing the danger for Beth.

Statistically, battering by an intimate partner is the single most frequent cause of injury to women in the United States. It is estimated that 22% to 35% of women seen in emergency rooms annually have been injured by battery. Yet the medical community has frequently failed to notice, comment on, or intervene in obvious cases of domestic violence. In the Sipe history, Beth was seen by numerous doctors for gross physical injuries, and not one appeared to question their source. Even when Sam slapped Daniel [Beth and Sam's son] in the presence of medical personnel, nothing was said or done to intervene.

The woman gets the message that no one cares about how she is abused and no one will help her. For the counselor hearing such stories, the task is to provide validation through empathy and a supportive atmosphere for the woman to release her pain and anger about such treatment.

When the Victim Is Treated as a Career Criminal

Counseling a battered woman after she has killed her abuser will often focus on the subject of her legal defense. In most cases, the woman is charged with first-degree murder, even though she has no past criminal record. Several issues immediately confront her.

One issue is how police have treated her. The treatment Beth received by the police on the night of the shooting and afterward is typical of experiences reported by other battered women who have killed in self-defense. Specifically, she was not allowed to take her purse, which resulted in theft of her money. She was not given medical attention even though she was clearly injured. She was given false information about the condition of her husband, and she was coerced to make a statement without counsel through false references to her son. When arrested and officially charged, she was subjected to strip searches and all the other indignities of incarceration. In short, Beth was treated as a career criminal. This treatment by the justice system when a woman acts in self-defense extends the wound created by the abuse.

The counselor is likely to observe the most severe symptoms of PTSD as the woman struggles to deal with her shame, degradation, terror, remorse, and anguish about all that has transpired. For example, Beth became anorexic and suicidal, both life-threatening conditions. The obvious solution of hospitalization had mixed results. The sense of safety along with individual and group therapy were helpful. However, "routine" medication, conclusions drawn from questionable testing, inconsistencies of treatment, use of the label of "murderer," and threats to commit her were damaging to her. At times, comments by the hospital personnel reflected more concern about Beth's legal status and their potential liability than about her mental health.

Thus, when considering hospitalization in such a case, the counselor needs to screen hospitals carefully for staff who are knowledgeable about domestic violence before recommending an inpatient facility.

The point of these observations is not to criticize the hospital, but rather to emphasize the need for specialized treatment of a battered woman suffering from acute PTSD. Such a patient needs a secure, supportive environment. She needs psychiatrists, nurses, and therapists who thoroughly understand domestic violence and the importance of empowerment in her treatment. She needs to be screened so that triggers which cause flashbacks can be identified and either avoided or removed. Above all, she needs continued, regular contact with her counselor and advocates throughout her hospital stay. As long as her legal case remains unresolved, the woman continues to live in the trauma and, therefore, to be at risk.

One alternative to hospitalizing a woman in Beth's situation is shelter placement. In a battered woman's shelter, she will have a secure, supportive environment with staff who are educated and experienced in dealing with domestic violence. However, the shelter will need to have the services of a psychiatrist to prescribe medication if necessary. After Beth's hospital experience, that component was arranged in cooperation with the local shelter.

Even in a protected atmosphere, the counselor must continue regular contact with the woman. The counselor can help to provide continuity, support, and advocacy, thereby helping the woman maintain a level of functioning high enough to survive the ordeal of defending herself in court.

Battered women also face paying for their legal defense counsel. This often taxes the financial resources of her entire family to the breaking point. The woman may work, sell off prized assets, or borrow money. In Beth's case, she used all three methods to raise money, including holding garage sales in which she sold some treasured items. Her financial crisis was intensified by bill collectors hounding her for payment of Sam's debts and by threats to foreclose on her house. These financial demands create more emotional stress for the woman, aggravating her already precarious emotional condition. Again, the counselor's focus is upon providing encouragement and support with reality testing as appropriate.

Protecting Her Children

Although concerns about her legal defense are constant, nothing may be as riveting for the battered woman who has killed as the welfare and future of her children. Often, the woman's perception that she is ensuring her children's welfare is a primary reason for her staying in the violent relationship.

Throughout her story, Beth demonstrates how strong this reason was for her. It is apparent how shattering the actions taken by social services were for her. The removal of her children from her care [after she was charged with murder] multiplied the impact of all her other traumas to the point that, for a brief period, she gave up hope and her will to struggle.

The counselor's role here is to interface with social service agencies when they are nonresponsive to the woman, without taking over for her. In Beth's case, this involved accompanying her to meet with a caseworker who did not return her phone calls.

Throughout counseling with a battered woman who has killed, the central focus should be on empowerment of the woman, and all techniques used should be consistent with this focus. The counselor must accept the woman's priorities and decisions as part of assisting her to become empowered.

The counselor's ability to maintain objectivity is of paramount importance and is likely to be challenging, particularly when involved in advocacy activities for the client.

ERASING THE SCARS OF ABUSE

Jennifer Bingham Hull

Jennifer Bingham Hull reports on Face to Face: The National Domestic Violence Project, which is sponsored by the American Academy of Facial Plastic and Reconstructive Surgery (AAFPRS) and the National Coalition Against Domestic Violence (NCADV). This program, Hull explains, provides battered women with free facial plastic surgery to repair the scars of domestic abuse that serve as constant reminders to many women even after they leave abusive relationships. Face to Face helps such women to reclaim their faces, restore damaged self-esteem, and put the past behind them, Hull asserts. However, not all battered women are candidates for plastic surgery, she cautions, because surgery should come at the end of the recovery process, after these women have addressed the emotional and psychological issues surrounding domestic abuse. Hull is a writer from Miami, Florida, who reports on women's issues and international affairs.

For years, Geni Hefner's face told the story.

It began with chicken dumplings. One night Hefner left the pan she'd used to make a sticky batch of dumplings in the sink to soak and went to sleep. The man she was then married to had a thing about cleanliness—any sign of dust or dirt sent him into a rage. Seeing the dirty pan in the sink upon returning home, he woke Hefner with a punch in the face, breaking her nose and leaving a huge jagged gash under her left eye with his wedding ring. Then he went to sleep. Bleeding profusely, Hefner drove herself to the local emergency room, where doctors sewed up her face with 16 stitches.

Scars Are a Constant Reminder

Hefner left her batterer in the late 1970s. In the years that followed she attempted to put her life back together, raising her two children on her own and working as an instructor and director at a modeling school. But she could never seem to put her violent seven-and-a-half-year marriage completely behind her. Every time she looked in the mirror, the jagged scar from that night, and an array of other marks from inci-

From Jennifer Bingham Hull, "After Abuse: Surgeons Help Erase the Scars," *Ms.*, January/February 1998. Reprinted by permission of *Ms.* magazine, ©1998.

dents like it, reminded her of the pain and degradation she'd experienced as a battered wife. Using makeup tricks from modeling, Hefner spent an hour each morning covering her scars with foundation and highlighter. "You get to the point where the makeup is automatic," says Hefner, who is in her late forties. "But still subconsciously you're constantly being reminded what put those scars there so that you have to wear more makeup. It's a constant, constant reminder of the past."

In March of 1996, Hefner finally had a chance to erase those years for good. In a six-hour operation at Houston's Methodist Hospital, Dr. Eugene Alford performed reconstructive plastic surgery on Hefner's face, giving her a face lift, brow lift, and eyelid lifts and resculpturing her cheeks (which had become sunken from beatings) with implants. Had Hefner been paying, the operation would have cost her at least $20,000. Instead, Alford and the hospital staff provided their services free.

For Hefner, the surgery capped a recovery process involving eight months of counseling, bringing her outer appearance into alignment with hard-won changes she'd made on the inside. These days, when she looks in the mirror, rather than confronting a woman who's been battered, she sees one who's been restored. "Now I go out without makeup. That's major, girl. I don't have to hide anything anymore," says Hefner, who runs her own video production company in Houston. The surgery has boosted Hefner's self-esteem and given her more confidence around people, helping her business. "It's like getting a new life. I look different. I feel different. I am different. The surgery is the final step to freedom. It's the final eraser."

Across the country more than 600 women who could not otherwise afford it have received free facial plastic surgery to repair everything from broken noses to battered brows through Face to Face: The National Domestic Violence Project. Sponsored by the American Academy of Facial Plastic and Reconstructive Surgery (AAFPRS) and the National Coalition Against Domestic Violence (NCADV), the program provides procedures ranging from simple scar corrections to complex operations costing up to $25,000 and requiring hospital stays. Some 273 plastic surgeons across the U.S. are participating in Face to Face. In communities like Houston, hospitals and specialists such as anesthesiologists are also donating thousands of dollars in services.

Reclaiming Their Faces

Many feminists, of course, are critical of the recent boom in cosmetic surgery for women, pointing out that it feeds society's notion that women must remain ageless and live up to unrealistic beauty standards. For battered women, however, plastic surgery can be far more than a cosmetic procedure. These patients say their facial scars have been a source of pain and embarrassment, often for years, their disfigured noses and smashed cheekbones serving as constant reminders of their former victimization. By reclaiming their faces, many feel they are removing their batterers' last hold on their lives. "It's wonderful to look in the mirror without my ex-husband staring me in the face," explains Hefner.

Oklahoma City plastic surgeon Lori Hansen was looking for a way to use her skills to express her strong Christian faith when she came up with the idea of serving domestic violence victims. Of the four to six million American women who are battered each year, more than one million require medical treatment. According to a Colorado study, some 75 percent of their injuries are to the face and head. Plastic surgeons have long served wealthy survivors of domestic violence, but their services are well beyond the means of many other battered women.

Working with her local shelter, Hansen began providing free surgery in 1992 to women who had been injured in domestic violence. A few years later, after Hansen presented her work to the board of AAFPRS, the organization established Face to Face in cooperation with NCADV.

Surgery Restores the Victim's Appearance

Women who call the Face to Face toll-free number are advised to meet with a local counselor who can provide a referral confirming that the woman's injuries are from domestic violence and that she's out of the abusive relationship. Face to Face aims to restore the victim's appearance to what it was before the battering. However, the line between reconstructive and cosmetic plastic surgery can be fuzzy, especially with women who've been abused. Frequent battering transforms the fat in the face into scar tissue, adding years to its victim's appearance. Cosmetic procedures, such as face lifts, are often performed to eliminate the cumulative effects of battering. In addition, the surgeons treat the direct effects of battering, fixing broken noses, smashed cheekbones, and crushed eye sockets. Some of the surgeries also correct ongoing physical ailments, such as breathing problems.

The surgeons' aim is to help restore battered women's self-esteem by erasing the physical evidence of their abuse. They see their contribution as coming at the end of the recovery process, after their patients have addressed the larger physical, emotional, and sheer survival issues that relate to battering.

While the program does not require women to go through counseling, many get extensive psychological help before surgery. The plastic surgeons emphasize that their procedures are no replacement for such inner work. "The corrective surgery is just one small piece to an enormous puzzle. These women's lives are shattered. They don't just have broken cheekbones, they have broken spirits. So you can't just do the Band-Aid therapy of repairing their physical injury, you have to fix their emotional injury," says Dr. George Brennan, the former president of AAFPRS who helped establish the program. "The psychological and spiritual repair has to precede the physical repair."

Many of Face to Face's patients say the surgery has brought them new confidence. Some found their facial scars from battering a constant source of humiliation. "It was like walking around with a sign on your face saying, 'I've been with an idiot,'" recalls a 32-year-old single mother in California who spent a year in a shelter where she received extensive counseling before getting her broken nose repaired by Brennan. "The surgery totally improved my whole outlook on my looks and my self. I feel like I just had a pair of battered shoes and now they're cleaned up. The past is over." Adds another of Brennan's Face to Face patients, whose husband kicked her face in with his cowboy boot a year after she left him: "The surgery was one of the final pieces in the recovery process. Now working with my kids is the rest of it."

Putting the Past Behind Them

Surgeons who work in Face to Face say just seeking the surgery can be a positive sign, indicating that the woman feels she deserves to look better again and wants to put the past behind her. It also takes courage. For Geni Hefner, being screened for Face to Face meant dredging up a nightmare she'd buried for 15 years. "The hardest thing I've ever done is drive up to the Houston Area Women's Center and get out of my car," she recalls of the eight months of counseling she received prior to surgery. Before her operation, Hefner carefully studied her face in a mirror and drew a map for Alford detailing every one of her 14 scars from battering. "It was like reliving every punch," she says.

These experiences have fueled Hefner's determination to avoid relationships with domineering men. "I went through such pain to get those scars," she says, "and I had to go through a lot of pain to get rid of the scars. I'm not about to let anybody mess my head or mind up again."

By reclaiming their faces, other women have taken charge of their lives for the first time in years.

Jane Stanley was watching television one night when an advertisement for Face to Face came on the air. The women featured had had facial scars from battering that looked much like her own. "I sat up in bed and said: 'That's it! I want that,'" recalls Stanley.

Stanley's face bore all the evidence of a 16-year-long abusive relationship. The mother of two had a thick scar from her eyebrow to the tip of her nose from the time her boyfriend shoved her head into the bathroom sink. He'd split her lips open, leaving a trail of scars around her mouth, and given her so many black eyes that the skin on her brow had sagged to cover her eyelids. Though the boyfriend had moved out, Stanley still felt his grip every time she looked in the mirror. "He said several times that he would always be part of my life because of all the scars he did to my face," says Stanley, who lives in Morehead City, North Carolina. "That's why I had such a gut feeling that I had to do this. I got rid of him and I wanted his hands off my face."

Coming Out of Hiding

In September of 1996, facial plastic surgeon Dr. Cynthia Gregg removed the excess skin and puffy tissue around Stanley's eyes, revised the deep scar across her face, and smoothed those around her mouth with laser skin resurfacing. Gregg says the surgery brightened Stanley's appearance. But she's been even more impressed by her patient's radical change in attitude. For years Stanley hid from the world, wearing her hair in bangs and down in front of her face to cover her scars, and avoiding people. "Before, I never looked someone in the eye because I knew that they were looking at my scars," says Stanley, who went through several months of counseling at a local shelter prior to her operation. "Now I look them straight in the eye and smile. The surgery has helped me do a 360-degree turnaround."

For Stanley, just getting the surgery was empowering. Before, her life focused on her boyfriend's needs. "If I had a dollar he got it," she recalls. Going to a counselor, tracking down a doctor who would do the surgery pro bono, and getting the operation meant standing up for herself. "This is my baby, my project. I investigated it. I found it. I got it. Getting the surgery made me realize I have a backbone," she says. A month after her surgery, the woman who could barely look people in the eye a year earlier spoke to 600 surgeons at a Face to Face fund-raiser in Washington, D.C. She now works at the battered women's shelter that initially helped her. "I can look in the mirror and I don't see anything holding me back there. I don't see any hands," she says. "I'm coming out."

Initially, participating surgeons feared they would be swamped with women seeking free surgery. Instead, many are frustrated that they aren't seeing more patients. Domestic violence victims are hard to reach, often living in isolation from society and lying about their injuries in the emergency room. And some doctors feel the shelters have not done enough to inform their clients about Face to Face. "The shelters have not been very receptive," says Dr. Edwin Williams, a facial plastic surgeon in Albany, New York. "They look at it as a mixed blessing. They're understaffed and underfunded. They look at it as one more project."

Certainly many shelters are overworked. However, several queried for this article said that while they thought the plastic surgery program could benefit some women and was a generous offer, they either didn't know much about it or felt their clients were too close to crisis to take advantage of it. "We tend to see the people who are hurting, who would be bad risks for surgery at this point. Maybe two years down the road they wouldn't be, but by then we don't know where they are," explains Kathleen Magee, director of domestic violence services at Equinox, a community services agency in Albany. Magee points out that what her clients need most are primary care doctors and legal aid.

Some Face to Face clients have unrealistic expectations about what surgery can do for them. In 1996, a 25-year-old woman came to Alford for pro bono surgery. The woman had documented evidence that she'd been separated from her previous abuser for a year and had been through counseling in a Houston shelter. A therapist had screened her. When the doctor asked her about her new boyfriend she said the relationship was great. Then she added: "My twisted nose is ugly. Maybe if I'm not ugly anymore he won't hit me." Sensing that the woman was back in another abusive situation, Alford told her she wasn't a candidate for surgery and advised her to get more counseling. "Straightening out your nose is not going to stop the abuse," he cautioned her.

Long-Term Results

It's impossible to know how many women treated in Face to Face have been reinjured. Surgeons participating in the program say these patients frequently skip their follow-up appointments, making it difficult to track what happens to them after the procedures. "If we had to do a scientific study on what we do—does it really work—I don't think any of us could quantify it scientifically because we have the same experience with a lot of these patients: they come and go and you never hear about them again," says Dr. Carlos Wolf, a facial plastic surgeon in Miami, Florida.

However, in the cases where the women do keep in touch, their stories of recovery can be inspiring. Jane Stanley has sent a steady stream of letters to Gregg since her surgery. In one she described how having her face restored had helped give her the confidence to look her abuser in the eye for the first time in the last of many encounters in court.

"He said I couldn't get his hands off my face, and look at my face—they're gone," says Stanley. "I got his hands off my face and I'm smiling!"

FAMILIES AND FRIENDS MUST RECOGNIZE THE DANGER

Susan Brewster

In the following selection, taken from her book *To Be an Anchor in the Storm: A Guide for Families and Friends of Abused Women*, Susan Brewster describes some of the signs of an abusive relationship that friends and family members may notice. A psychotherapist who was also once a battered woman, Brewster points out that victims of abuse face a precarious life and may behave erratically or unpredictably. These women may not always present a realistic picture of their relationship and may even defend their abuser, the author stresses. However, friends or family members who suspect abuse must take steps to help, because a woman in an abusive relationship is in danger of losing her life, Brewster concludes.

It can be very difficult to be a friend or relative of an abused woman. The more you care for her the more emotionally difficult it can be for you, even if you are not in contact with her. If you don't yet know for a fact that your loved one is abused but you suspect it, your relationship with her is probably strained. You might sense something is wrong in her relationship with her partner but don't have solid evidence that they're involved in something as stigmatizing as domestic violence. You might also find yourself feeling frustrated and confused by your loved one's behavior. You may notice that she tends to contradict herself and tells stories about her relationship that conflict with one another. One day she boasts that her partner is the most wonderful father, while the next she complains of his quick temper with the kids. One moment she tells you that no one has ever made her feel so special. Then she complains that he belittles her in front of his friends.

Living a Precarious Life

If you know for a fact that a woman whom you care about is being abused, it is probably bothering you at some level, whether or not you are admitting it to yourself. You might also find yourself confused. You may hear that he has stopped hitting her only to discover later that he is keeping her up arguing at night to the point where she is too exhausted to keep her job. Even more frustrating is that she may seem rather flighty herself. You might wonder how seriously you should take her hints about her partner's abuse if she can't hold a rational thought in her head, or hold a job, or keep her life in better order.

Let's face it, an abused woman can seem, to the average person, pretty unstable! She can be forgetful, her thoughts scattered. Her behavior can be very erratic. She might seem depressed or ill-tempered, nervous or withdrawn. She might not follow through with things she plans to do, or keep promises. She might act as if she prefers to be left alone. Or, she might seem to be none of those things. She might come across as the epitome of emotional strength and personal success. Most likely, if you knew her before she met her abuser, she has gradually but significantly changed. At one time she may have been vibrant and lively; now she is lethargic and preoccupied. You may not understand why or how she got to be so out of balance. You just know that you don't like to be around her much anymore.

An abused woman leads a very precarious life. One minute she is held out by her partner as the angel of his universe, while the next minute she's groveling at his feet like a whipped puppy, begging him to stop hitting her. One day he gives her flowers and a new car. The next day he stomps on the flowers and throws her car keys in the river. One week he does all the housework and takes the kids out so she can have some time alone. The next week he tells her that she's a sloppy housekeeper and a neglectful mother. One year (yes, there can be that much time between abusive incidents!) he's getting along with everyone at work and seems to be making friends. The next year he quits job after job and hangs out at the local bar getting in fights and losing grocery money on bets at the pool table. Is it any wonder that an abused woman becomes confused and depressed? Anyone would!

Blaming the Battered Woman

You might think that in some ways she causes her abuse. Many people involved in the life of a battered woman assume that, at the very least, she is responsible for deciding to stay with her partner after the abuse has begun. Statements I have heard from various people run the gamut: "I would leave a guy in a minute if he did that to me." "She must like it at some level or she wouldn't stay with him." "I have no sympathy for people who don't *do* something to change their situations." "There's no way she's battered, she's just as tough as he is." "But she's a lawyer! She's too smart to let some guy hurt her."

Perhaps you agree with some of these statements. If you do, you're not alone. In my experience most people hold some of these beliefs before they learn any facts about the issues surrounding domestic violence. Indeed, these are very common beliefs shared by people of many different backgrounds. I have even been shocked to hear a few of these statements made by members of my own family who knew about my own abuse experience! There are obviously some very pervasive beliefs about domestic abuse in our society, so pervasive that even victims of abuse sometimes believe them.

Often, battered women are as confused as anyone about their own motives for staying with their abusive partner. Upon first entering counseling or a battered women's shelter, many women I have worked with have made statements like: "I must be crazy to still love him." "Why am I not strong enough to leave like other women that this happens to?" "I can't believe I'm going back to him after what he did to me this time." As a result of this confusion and self-blame, battered women often feel extremely ashamed and embarrassed. Then they become even *more* isolated and secretive, particularly with regard to those people who care about them most. Even if they do talk with friends or family about the abuse, they usually make it sound much less serious than it really is.

Recognizing the Danger

Perhaps the woman you are concerned about doesn't make her relationship with her partner sound very bad; therefore, you might assume it isn't. She describes her partner as having a "bad temper" or says that he gets "kind of crazy" at times. Or maybe she uses statements like "He blew up" or "He lost it" when she describes an argument with him. You might be thinking, doesn't everyone get mad sometimes and have arguments? Does that necessarily mean that there is physical abuse? And even if he pushes and shoves her a little during fights, does that automatically make someone a batterer? Anyway, all couples have problems, don't they? Troubled times pass. It isn't your business. Right? Besides, her behavior and his might seem so irrational that it begins to feel like you're watching a soap opera on television. You might decide that you have enough to worry about in your own life, that you don't need to be stressed out further with this continuous "melodrama."

Still, you may have a nagging voice inside telling you that there could be more to this than meets the eye, that possibly you could help if you just knew how. This could really be dangerous for her, like the stories in the news in which a man stalks his ex-wife and kills her, or stories about a husband getting more cruel and torturous over the years and finally snapping one day, killing his family and then himself.

It is important for you to understand that *you are probably allowed to see only the very tip of the iceberg which represents her abusive relationship.* And what you do see is probably extremely skewed. When battered women choose to share information about their abuse with someone, they rarely present it in a complete and realistic way. They might minimize it to the extent that an all-day beating is presented as a minor "blowup." Nevertheless, despite the minimizations and distortions, it is possible to move yourself into a position where the woman you are concerned about shares enough for your suspicions to be confirmed or denied.

So, you can't necessarily gauge how seriously to take her situation by how she presents it, and even though you may only suspect that she is abused, the price of not confirming your suspicions is probably higher than you think. Are you prepared to sit back and do nothing when there may be a threat to her very existence? I'm writing to tell you, with all my conviction and experience, *her life is in danger* if she is in a battering relationship. She could die at the hands of this man who supposedly loves her.

If you are confused, imagine how confused *she* must be. If you still want to help, you can! But only if you are willing to unlearn the myths, unfeel some very natural feelings, and fight against some very basic instincts. In other words, you must change yourself!

CHAPTER 3

LEGAL ISSUES

CRIMINAL JUSTICE MEASURES

National Research Council

In 1995, Congress asked the National Research Council, a federally funded think tank in Washington, D.C., to develop a research agenda designed to increase understanding of violence against women. In response to the congressional request, the Council established a Panel on Research on Violence Against Women. Excerpted from the panel's 1996 report, the following selection provides an overview of the criminal justice measures available to protect battered women from their abusers. The report examines various methods, including mandatory arrest policies, protective orders, court-mandated counseling for batterers, and coordinated community responses. The panel also reports on research concerning the effectiveness of some of these measures.

Throughout U.S. history, women's advocates have sought laws and law enforcement to prevent violence against women. The modern women's movement succeeded in bringing federal attention to the problem in the 1970s. In 1984 the U.S. Attorney General's Task Force on Family Violence published recommendations for justice system action and for needed research on family violence, including battering against women. More recently, the Violence Against Women Act of the Violent Crime Control and Law Enforcement Act of 1994 promotes a number of efforts in the criminal justice arena, such as arrest of batterers and those who violate protective orders; coordination of police, prosecutor, and judicial responsibilities for battering cases; and coordination of computer tracking systems for communication among police, prosecutors, and courts.

Pressure for Change
The women's movement in the 1970s called not only for the creation of services for women who had suffered violent victimization, but also for the criminal justice system to treat rape and battering as it did other crimes. This call entailed pressure for changes in laws, particularly with respect to rape, and better enforcement of the laws pertaining to all forms of violence against women. Interest in treatment for

sex offenders and batterers also grew during the 1970s and 1980s.

A growing body of research has examined the impact of criminal justice interventions. There is mixed evidence about the ability of various criminal justice interventions to protect individual women or change individual men's behavior. The impact on the rate of battering or sexual assault at the community level remains unknown. In discussing criminal justice responses, it must be remembered that there really is not a single criminal justice system in the United States; rather, there are at least 51 models, determined by state and federal laws, and numerous other practices associated with local jurisdictions. . . .

The Minneapolis Domestic Violence Experiment

Whether or not police should arrest perpetrators on the scene of batterings tends to dominate the discussions of appropriate police interventions. Warrantless arrest has been the subject of extensive research to evaluate its effectiveness in preventing battering. The Minneapolis Domestic Violence Experiment pioneered the use of randomized designs to compare the consequences of arrest to alternative police actions. In the Minneapolis experiment, police officers' discretion was replaced with randomized treatments of arrest, separation, or offering advice before leaving the victim and offender together. Arrest was found to result in a reduced chance of new violence within the next 6 months. These findings encouraged many jurisdictions across the country to institute either mandatory or presumptive warrantless arrest for battering cases.

Attempts to replicate the Minneapolis findings have resulted in less clear-cut outcomes. Known collectively as SARP (the Spouse Assault Replication Program of the National Institute of Justice), experiments testing arrest and alternative police interventions were performed in Omaha, Nebraska, Charlotte, North Carolina, Milwaukee, Wisconsin, Dade County, Florida, and Colorado Springs, Colorado. Because the experimental designs differed among the sites, comparing results proved difficult and confusing. In 1995, J. Garner, J. Fagan, and C. Maxwell reanalyzed the data for comparative purposes and concluded that arrest was no better or worse than other police actions much of the time. When arrest did make a difference, it reduced the chance of new violence relative to alternative police treatments. Contrary to some interpretations, Garner, Fagan, and Maxwell found no reliable evidence that arrest increases the likelihood of repeat violence; rather, it may be less effective in decreasing violence than other practices. However, if arrest is an option, one must wonder if the failure to arrest is perceived by a batterer as implicit permission to continue his violent behavior.

The experience with the arrest studies indicates how difficult it can be to convert even well-designed studies into policy recommendations. The initial Minneapolis findings were widely circulated and led

to arrest policies in many jurisdictions, even after the replication studies were less supportive of arrest. Making policy on the basis of one
unreplicated study can be risky, but research is not the only impetus
for policy. It may be that the Minneapolis results simply reinforced
other social pressures at the time, such as successful lawsuits against
police departments that had failed to respond to battering incidents.

Measuring Results Is Difficult

As in evaluations of services for victims, controversies arise over what
outcomes should be measured and how to measure them. One may
wish to measure subsequent violence, but the use of official records
may not give an accurate portrayal of new incidents of violence. Victims may not report repeat violence to police for a number of reasons,
including dissatisfaction with the police handling of the case. Estimates from National Crime Victimization Survey data indicate that
only 56 percent of battering incidents are reported to police. Other
research has estimated that as few as 7 percent to 14 percent of battering incidents are reported. When victims are pleased with police
response, they may be more likely to report repeat violence. In either
event, what is being measured is not repeat violence, but willingness
to call the police. Reliance on interviews with victims may catch
repeat incidents of violence that were not reported to police, but victims are often difficult to locate or may not want to be interviewed.
For example, of the 330 cases in the Omaha experiment, 67 (20.3 percent) of the women did not complete initial interviews and an additional 21 women (6.4 percent) could not be located for 6-month
follow-up interviews. Another issue in outcome measurement is how
long the follow-up period should be.

Apart from the question of specific prevention, it remains to be
demonstrated that arrest is a general deterrent to battering. K.R.
Williams and R. Hawkins analyzed perceptual data from males interviewed as part of the second National Family Violence Survey to test
the relative effects of formal and informal controls on potential
aggression. They found that the greatest deterrent effect was associated with informal controls implied by moral disapproval of assault and
by social attachments. A lesser, but significant, general deterrent oper-
ated through the perceived risk of arrest. Assuming that the perceived
risk is enhanced by knowledge of actual arrests when police respond
to incidents of battering, one can expect a proarrest policy to inform
and then deter men who would be inclined to batter. There may be
differential deterrence effects of arrest among various groups of men.
For example, the extremely high arrest and incarceration rate (for all
crimes) among urban African American young men may make arrest
less of a deterrent for them. Yet African American women are more
likely than white women to call the police, and African American
men are more likely than white men to be arrested.

Prosecution Policies Vary

In jurisdictions that have not paid special attention to or were apparently not concerned about domestic violence, prosecution rates of battering cases typically have been low. In jurisdictions that are supportive of criminal justice interventions for domestic violence, prosecution rates have been higher.

Whether a case begins through arrest or a victim-initiated complaint, it is the prosecutor's office that acts as the gatekeeper in bringing a case to the courts. There is great variety across the country in policies pertaining to prosecution of battering cases. Some jurisdictions encourage victim-initiated complaints, while others discourage or outright refuse to prosecute such cases. There is some evidence to suggest that allowing victim-initiated complaints serves a protective function for the victim. D. Ford found a decrease in violence of at least 47 percent for any victim-initiated complaint policy, according to victim interview reports of incidents before and after prosecution.

A major issue in prosecution is whether or not a victim should be allowed to drop the charges. In general, it has been assumed that prosecution can only protect victims under policies meant to keep victims in the criminal justice system while state power is used to control offenders. Foremost among recommended policies is a "no-drop" policy, promoted as making it impossible for a defendant to pressure a victim to drop charges, thereby possibly protecting the victim from coercive violence. Furthermore, a no-drop policy signifies that the prosecution is committed to acting against battering, which may serve as a general deterrent. Others argue that a no-drop policy disempowers victims who may be able to use the possibility of dropping charges to negotiate self-protective arrangements. Findings from the Indianapolis Domestic Violence Prosecution Experiment revealed that a victim who was permitted to drop charges and whose defendant had been arrested on a warrant had the lowest chance of suffering new violence within 6 months of the case's being settled. There is an important difference between a policy of allowing charges to be dropped and the actual dropping of charges. Ford also found that women who were permitted to drop charges and did so were no better off than those whose cases were prosecuted under a no-drop policy.

Protective Orders

Protective orders include any of a number of court orders demanding that a potentially dangerous suspect stay away from an identified individual. Typical orders include restraining orders issued in the course of a civil matter, orders of protection issued at the request of a victim who feels endangered, and no-contact orders issued by a criminal court during its proceedings or as a condition of probation. The terms of a protective order can vary from no violent contact to no contact whatsoever with the petitioner, her friends, coworkers, etc. Orders may specify terms of child visitation or use of property. Most states today have criminalized the violation of protection orders and give police officers the authority to make warrantless arrests for their violation.

The Violence Against Women Act of 1994 created a new crime of crossing a state line to violate a protective order. The law also gives full faith and credit to protective orders, so that an order issued in one state must be enforced in another state. Whether or not this federal law improves the enforcement of protection orders will depend in large part on how local police coordinate with federal authorities in enforcement.

A few studies have addressed the effectiveness of protective orders in preventing violence. All are limited in their findings by problems in implementing and enforcing their terms. In multiple sites around the United States, J. Grau, J. Fagan, and S. Wexler found that, although victims felt protective orders to be effective, there was no difference in rates of victimization between those with and without orders. Indeed, the study revealed evidence that protective orders may aggravate violence when they are not enforced by the police. E.S. Buzawa and C.G. Buzawa report that samples of police in Massachusetts rarely arrested people even when they had probable cause to act against violations of protective orders. A. Harrell, B. Smith, and L. Newmark found that protective orders in Denver and Boulder were effective for at least a year in preventing violence against the petitioners in comparison with victims without orders. In other respects, however, the orders were largely ineffective: 75 percent of offenders contacted the victims and 21 percent stalked them. As in other studies, arrest for violations was rare, and, thus, compromised the potential of a protective order for preventing violence.

Judicial Discretion

Judges and judicial processing are the least studied aspects of criminal justice, yet judges' discretion and court procedures can have profound effects on the actions of other parts of the criminal justice system and on victim safety. For example, K.J. Ferraro found that judges in Phoenix were critical of police who made arrests under the department's presumptive arrest policy, and, therefore, police were reluctant to make arrests.

Judges' decisions can directly affect battering cases: judges can determine pretrial release conditions, such as whether or not a defendant should be released, how long he should be held prior to release, the nature and amount of bond, and whether a protective order should be issued. In victim-initiated cases, judges decide whether to issue a warrant for the man's arrest or a summons for his appearance. During the course of a trial, judges make decisions about continuances and the types of evidence that will be allowed. If a defendant is found guilty, judges often exercise considerable discretion in sentencing. Little research exists on the effects of these various judicial decisions. In response to low rates of prosecution for batterers, some jurisdictions have created special courts to deal with cases involving intimate partner violence. Although no evaluations have been completed on the effects of such courts, the Dade County (Florida) Domestic Violence Court is currently being evaluated using an experimental design to see if legal sanctions are more likely and more severe under this system and if victims and their children are safer.

The Verdict Is Not in on Counseling

Court-mandated counseling for batterers is a popular option from the perspective of both victims and criminal justice practitioners. It satisfies victims' interests that batterers receive help and seems to give judges a feeling of constructive action to rehabilitate offenders. L.K. Hamberger and J.E. Hastings describe two primary types of court mandates. The first is pretrial diversion, whereby the batterer can have his arrest record cleared or the charge reduced on successful completion of treatment. The second is a direct court order to participate in treatment as part of a sentence imposed after conviction. Little research has been done on the effect of court mandates on treatment completion or on whether sanctions are imposed for noncompliance.

One study of court-mandated treatment found that men who completed the program were significantly more likely to have been in treatment by court order. About two-thirds of the court-mandated treatment group completed treatment, compared with about two-fifths of men whose treatment was not court ordered. D.G. Saunders and J.C. Parker found that other factors may have also been at work. In their study, younger, less well-educated men were more likely to complete treatment if it was court ordered; men over 25 with college educations were more likely to complete treatment if it was voluntary. Saunders and Parker also looked at the type of court mandate. Although significant differences in rates of attrition from treatment were not found, there was a trend for those men with deferred prosecution to have greater completion rates.

Much remains unknown about the impact of court-mandated treatment. Of particular concern is the effect of court-mandated treatment on reducing violent behavior. A few studies have found lower recidivism (as measured by repeat arrests) among men whose treatment was court mandated in comparison with men who received other court sanctions. However, A. Harrell found higher recidivism among men in court-mandated treatment than among those in a nontreatment group.

Coordinated Community Responses

As changes came about in various components of the criminal justice system, both battered women's advocates and their colleagues in the various parts of the justice system recognized a need for more coordinated efforts. Multiple models of coordinated community approaches have been developed, including community intervention projects, coordinating councils, community partnering, technical assistance projects, and community organizing. Community intervention projects have been the most evaluated of the various models. These projects involve a grassroots organization that sets up procedures with the local criminal justice agencies to establish and monitor policies related to battering, to be informed of batterers' arrests so that advocates can be provided to the battered woman to help her navigate the legal system and locate services for herself and her children, and to provide information on batterers' treatment options to the arrested man.

Although initial evaluations seem to indicate that coordinated community efforts may decrease repeat violence, research is sparse. D.J. Gamache, J.L. Edleson, and M.D. Schock retrospectively studied three communities in which community intervention projects had been established. Using archival police and court records, they found that the projects had a significant impact on increasing the levels of arrests for battering, convictions, and court mandates to treatment. In a comparison of cases of battering that occurred prior to the establishment of a coordinated community effort to those after it was established, M. Steinman found that arrests prior to the coordinated effort increased repeat violence, while police action, particularly arrest, in coordination with other criminal justice efforts deterred further violence. M. Syers, and J.L. Edleson collected data on all woman abuse cases during a 13-month period in two police precincts in Minneapolis. Besides looking at official police and legal advocate records, they interviewed as many female victims as could be reached by telephone contact immediately following the police visit and 6 and 12 months later. At 12 months they found a trend for the least repeat violence among men who were arrested and ordered to treatment followed by the men who were arrested and not ordered to treatment with the highest repeat violence among men who were not arrested.

Coordinated community responses that involve activities other than domestic violence programs and the criminal justice system have not been evaluated. Many practitioners recognize the need for interactions and coordination among various systems that might intervene with victims and offenders. The Violence Against Women Act of 1994 includes demonstration grants for coordinating domestic violence programs with the criminal justice system, the social service system, the health care and mental health systems, the education community, the religious community, the business community, and other pertinent community groups and activities.

FEDERAL PROTECTION: THE VIOLENCE AGAINST WOMEN ACT

Johanna R. Shargel

In response to testimony and evidence concerning the burden that gender-motivated violence places on the national economy and the failure of state systems to protect women from violence, in 1994 Congress passed the Violence Against Women Act (VAWA), creating a federal civil rights remedy for victims of gender-motivated violence. In the following selection, Johanna R. Shargel explores the reasoning behind the development of the VAWA civil rights remedy. Some states still have laws that make it difficult for women to obtain protection or justice, she writes. Furthermore, Shargel argues, many police officers, prosecutors, and judges discriminate against women in domestic violence cases. She also asserts that other civil rights laws, which were primarily designed to combat racism, are insufficient to address the problem of battered women because, unlike racial discrimination, violence against women occurs privately. A federal remedy is necessary, the author concludes, so that women will receive equal protection under the law. At the time this selection was written, Shargel was a law student at Yale University.

Violence currently poses the most significant threat to women's rights as equal citizens. The Senate Judiciary Committee, after reviewing a wide array of studies on violence against women in the United States, reported in 1993 that "[v]iolence is the leading cause of injuries to women ages 15 to 44, more common than automobile accidents, muggings, and cancer deaths combined." Violence against women occurs with disturbing frequency and results in severe, often fatal, injuries. A 1995 Department of Justice survey reported that, in total, women aged twelve and older annually sustain almost five million violent victimizations. . . .

Until recently, women victimized by the reality or threat of violence were left without an effective remedy, and therefore denied their right to full and equal citizenship. First, the disabling physical

Reprinted by permission of The Yale Law Journal Company and Fred B. Rothman & Company from "In Defense of the Civil Rights Remedy of the Violence Against Women Act," by Johanna R. Shargel, *The Yale Law Journal*, vol. 106, pp. 1849–83.

and psychological effects of violence have kept women from participating as commercial actors, and their absence from the nation's mar-
ketplace has had a substantial effect on interstate commerce. Women
have, in Sally Goldfarb's [Senior Staff Attorney, the National Organization for Women (NOW) Legal Defense and Education Fund] words,
been "relegated to a form of second-class citizenship" because violence has prevented them from contributing to the national economy
on an equal footing with men. Women have also been "relegated to a
form of second-class citizenship" because state criminal justice systems have frequently denied female victims of violence their right to
equal protection of the laws. Because both the restrictive letter and
the biased implementation of state laws have failed to keep women
"safe at home or on the streets," women continually have been
deprived of their full citizenship rights.

The Violence Against Women Act

In September 1994, Congress passed the Violence Against Women Act
(VAWA), drafted in response to what its chief legislative sponsor, Senator Joseph R. Biden, called a "national tragedy." The law evolved gradually over a four-year period during which Congress heard testimony
from women's rights and civil rights organizations, state attorneys
general, law professors, law enforcement officials, physicians, and victims of violence. What emerged from this expert testimony is a comprehensive statute containing a wide range of provisions designed to
address the pressing problem of violence against women.

For example, to improve overall safety for women, the VAWA
increases penalties for federal rape convictions and provides state
grants to support law enforcement and educational efforts aimed at
reducing violent crime against women. With respect to domestic violence, the Act criminalizes interstate domestic violence, and ensures
that a protective order issued in one state is given "full faith and credit" in all other states. In an effort to achieve equal justice for women
in the courts, the Act authorizes grants to improve the training of
judges who deal with issues involving domestic violence and also
encourages circuit judicial councils to conduct gender bias studies.

Without question, the most controversial provision of the VAWA is
the section entitled "Civil Rights for Women." This provision estab-
lishes a federal civil rights cause of action for victims of violent crimes
"motivated by gender." The Civil Rights Remedy defines a violent
crime as any act that would be a federal or state felony, whether or
not the offense has actually resulted in criminal charges, prosecution,
or conviction. Under the statute, a person who commits a crime of
gender-motivated violence, whether a public or private actor, is liable
to the injured party and subject to compensatory and punitive damages, as well as injunctive and declaratory relief.

The VAWA Civil Rights Remedy is based on two independent constitutional sources of legislative authority: the Commerce Clause and the Fourteenth Amendment's enforcement provision, Section Five. . . .

Voluminous testimony at the congressional hearings on the VAWA Civil Rights Remedy evidenced the tremendous strain that violence against women imposes on the nation's productive capacity, clearly demonstrating that gender-motivated violence has a substantial effect on interstate commerce. As the Senate Judiciary Committee summarized: "Gender-based crimes and the fear of gender-based crimes restrict movement, reduce employment opportunities, increase health expenditures, and reduce consumer spending, all of which affect interstate commerce and the national economy." Extensive congressional findings and other studies demonstrate that gender-motivated violence has a detrimental effect on interstate commerce.

Violence Against Women Threatens the Economy

First, gender-motivated violence severely limits women's contribution to the national economy. Over thirty years ago, when enacting Title VII of the 1964 Civil Rights Act, Congress sought to guarantee equal opportunity for women in employment. Gender-motivated violence, however, defeats the purpose and benefit of Title VII; it physically prevents millions of American women from full participation in commercial activity. Domestic violence in particular significantly impairs job performance: Victims of domestic violence are often harassed by their batterers at work, prevented from arriving to work on time, and kept from attending work altogether because of serious injuries. Moreover, the threat of violence affects women's employment decisions and conduct to a large extent: Fear of violence deters women from applying for or accepting job positions in unsafe neighborhoods, and it discourages women from working after dark or on weekends. The fear and threat of violence affect every American woman and therefore have both an inevitable and an enormous impact on interstate commerce.

Gender-motivated violence not only deprives women of employment opportunities, but also has a significant effect on business nationwide. At the VAWA congressional hearings, experts on abuse and legal scholars described how gender-motivated violence depletes the nation's workforce. As New York University law professor Burt Neuborne explained:

> In pure economic terms, the sheer loss of productivity attributable to violent gender-based assault is staggering. . . . The dislocation of the nation's labor force that is caused by fear of violent gender-based assault is enormous: women who do not enter or who leave the labor force because of fear; women whose choice of job is dictated by fear; women whose performance on the job is affected by fear.

Due to the prevalence of violence against women, employers across the country must contend with lost productivity, increased health-care and security costs, and higher turnover.

In addition to decreasing nationwide production, violence against women also has a negative effect on levels of commercial consumption. As one witness explained at the VAWA congressional hearings:

> Women who cannot traverse public streets without fear will also not use places of public accommodation, purchase goods, or conduct business in such areas. Fear of gender-motivated violence restricts the hours during which women can engage in a variety of activities and seriously curtails their participation in the commerce of our nation.

Whether analyzing the economic loss precipitated by gender-motivated violence from the perspective of supply or demand, the conclusion is the same: Gender-motivated violence affects interstate commerce because women as a group constitute approximately half the nation's consumers and producers. The fact that the VAWA Civil Rights Remedy is rooted in the Commerce Clause rightly acknowledges that when half the citizens of this country—half the commercial actors—either fear or are subject to incapacitation by violence because of their gender, the entire nation suffers. . . .

In addition to the Commerce Clause, Congress relied on Section Five of the Fourteenth Amendment as a constitutional basis for the VAWA Civil Rights Remedy. Section Five provides that "Congress shall have power to enforce, by appropriate legislation, the provisions" of the Fourteenth Amendment. In this instance, Congress aimed to enforce Section One of the Fourteenth Amendment, which states that, "[n]o State shall . . . deny to any person within its jurisdiction the equal protection of the laws." Congress invoked Section Five because it aimed to provide victims of gender-motivated violence with equal protection of the laws where state systems had failed. . . .

Inequality in the State System

Congress enacted the VAWA Civil Rights Remedy based on an extensive legislative record that documented the many ways in which state courts do not afford female crime victims equal protection of the laws as guaranteed by Section One of the Fourteenth Amendment. Gender bias and discrimination within the state system frequently deprive women of the protection to which they are entitled. As Senator Biden described the problem on introducing the VAWA Remedy to Congress: "[I]t is still easier to convict a car thief than a rapist, and authorities are more likely to arrest a man for parking tickets than for beating his wife. . . ."

Obstacles to equal treatment for female victims of violence within the state system exist at both legal and administrative levels. On a legal level, state statute books are rife with formal bars to equality. For example, some states still retain a marital exemption to laws prohibiting rape; several states also heighten the legal standards for proving sexual assault against cohabitants and dating companions. Another legal barrier to equality is the interspousal immunity doctrine, which in some states still prevents battered women from suing their husbands to recover damages for either medical expenses or pain and suffering. Strict statutes of limitations, yet another legal obstacle in some states, pose particular problems for young victims of sexual assault, who permanently lose their opportunity to pursue a civil remedy if they fail to bring suit within a few years of the attack. . . .

These legal barriers to equality are compounded by discriminatory administrative practices, which undermine whatever protection is provided by the letter of state law. Congressional hearings on the VAWA Remedy showed that gender bias contaminates every level of the state system, and that insensitive and unresponsive treatment by police, prosecutors, and judges often results in low reporting and conviction rates. Police, responsible for the initial screening of cases, are notorious for not responding to situations involving violence against women, particularly domestic violence. . . .

State Laws Are Not Enforced

Equally problematic is the well-documented fact that prosecutors often fail to enforce vigorously laws prohibiting gender-motivated violence. As one commentator described: "Faced with limited time, personnel, and resources . . . prosecutors often give domestic violence cases low priority and sometimes I even try to persuade battered women not to prosecute." At the congressional hearings on the Civil Rights Remedy, it was readily apparent that prosecutors across the country either refuse to charge or significantly undercharge alleged perpetrators of sex crimes:

> Witnesses told of counties in which no acquaintance rape prosecutions had been brought. . . . They quoted from Justice Department studies showing that most domestic violence cases caused injuries as serious as most felonies and, yet, experience demonstrated that most domestic violence crimes were charged as misdemeanors. They testified about threats to witnesses routinely prosecuted in drug cases but ignored in domestic abuse cases. . . .

Gender bias exists among state court judges as well. For example, the Washington State Task Force on Gender and Justice in the Courts reported that nearly one "quarter of the [state judges] believed that rape victims 'sometimes' or 'frequently' precipitate their sexual assaults because of what they wear and/or actions preceding the incidents." One state court judge told a domestic violence victim seeking protection in his court, "'Let's kiss and make up and get out of my court.'" The New York State Task Force found that some judges "shunt victims back and forth between police and family court until they give up seeking protection."

In the face of this evidence demonstrating that state justice systems discriminate against female victims of violence at every level, some remain convinced that state courts afford victims of gender-motivated violence equal protection of the laws. For example, one law professor has argued that because violence against women "is already adequately covered by state law," the VAWA Remedy is a "wasteful duplication of resources." Most critics, however, do not contest the extensive findings of widespread bias in the state court system, but instead argue that as an antidote to this inequity, the VAWA Civil Rights Remedy exceeds Congress's power under Section Five to enforce the Equal Protection Clause of the Fourteenth Amendment. . . .

The VAWA Remedies Equal Protection Problems

Several aspects of the VAWA Civil Rights Remedy illustrate the fact that the statute was specifically designed to remedy equal protection problems. First, the Remedy appropriately addresses the type of violence most frequently suffered by women. It is well established that most violence against women occurs in private and is perpetrated by people known to the victim. In contrast to race-based discrimination, acts of gender-motivated violence are not usually committed under color of state law or by a conspiracy of wrongdoers. Because existing civil rights laws were drafted primarily to address the problem of racial discrimination, these laws do not respond in any significant way to the problem of gender-motivated violence. As Representative Patricia Schroeder explained at the VAWA legislative hearings: "Gender motivated violence cannot be adequately affected by existing civil rights structures because gender crimes manifest themselves differently than other crimes—they tend to be acts by individuals." Clearly, a meaningful and effective civil rights remedy for victims of gender-motivated violence must reach violence committed by individuals acting in a private capacity. Because the VAWA Remedy is the first civil rights statute to recognize what constitutes the most common and devastating threat to women's equal citizenship, it is true to its purpose of enforcing the Equal Protection Clause.

The VAWA Civil Rights Remedy also effectively remedies the problem of equal protection at the state level by simply offering an alternative, less biased forum for victims of gender-motivated violence. First, plaintiffs bringing suit in federal court do not have to contend with unjust and outmoded laws, such as the marital rape exemption and the fresh complaint rule, which still exist in a number of states. Second, although gender discrimination undoubtedly exists in the federal system as well, there is evidence that female victims of violence have received fairer treatment in federal court. The very fact that the VAWA Civil Rights Remedy offers a federal forum for victims of gender-motivated violence, along with the fact that the Remedy specifically addresses the most frequent and harmful kind of violence against women, leads to the inevitable conclusion that the VAWA Remedy is "appropriate legislation" to further the aims of Section One of the Fourteenth Amendment.

The Civil Rights Remedy Is Necessary

Gender-motivated violence is a federal problem that warrants a federal solution. Although the constitutional bases of the VAWA Civil Rights Remedy have been and are expected to be fiercely contested, Congress most likely acted within its authority under both the Commerce Clause and Section Five of the Fourteenth Amendment. . . .

If gender-motivated violence continues unabated by a federal remedy, women will continue to be deprived of their full citizenship rights. State law as currently enforced does not provide victims of gender-motivated violence the full rights of citizenship; victims are frequently denied equal protection of the laws by many state criminal justice systems. Moreover, unassisted victims of violence cannot participate on an equal basis in the national economy; their contribution to interstate commerce decreases and consequently, in Sally Goldfarb's words, "our entire society is diminished." As two parts of the same equation, the Commerce Clause and Section Five bases of the VAWA Civil Rights Remedy are both necessary and appropriate means of achieving full and equal citizenship.

THE BATTERED WOMAN SYNDROME DEFENSE

Lenore Walker

Psychologist Lenore Walker is the author of *The Battered Woman Syndrome*, which examines the results of her study on the effects of battering. Walker suggests that some abused women develop Battered Woman Syndrome (BWS), which can significantly affect their judgment and memory. For instance, she writes, victims suffering from BWS find it difficult to tell the difference between memories of past abuse and current threats, making their experience of fear and their perception of danger even more intense. If a battered woman with these symptoms believes that violence is imminent, Walker argues, she may take actions to protect herself that she would not normally take, including killing her batterer. Walker explains that understanding BWS has helped the legal system to respond appropriately to victims of abuse.

It has been more than 15 years since I first testified as an expert witness using Battered Woman Syndrome (BWS) to explain the psychological state of mind of a woman who killed her abusive partner in self-defense. In that 1977 case, Miriam Grieg, a Billings, Montana, woman, called the police after shooting her husband six times as he lay in their bed. After beating her severely, he had thrown the gun at her, shouting, "If you don't shoot me, I will kill you with this gun." Accustomed to doing what he ordered for fear of further abuse, Miriam shot him with all the hollow-point bullets in the gun.

Before the police entered the bedroom, she warned them in what they later described as a terrified voice, "Be careful, he has a lot of guns in there. He's going to be very angry and will shoot you." Obviously, she didn't believe that he could have died, despite the devastating scene that lay behind that door.

Miriam was charged with murder. After hearing testimony about the psychological effects of battering, an all-woman jury in Yellowstone County, Montana, found her not guilty.

Meanwhile, in Washington, D.C., a soft-spoken, pregnant nurse named Beverly Ibn-Tamas had shot and killed her husband when he

Reprinted, with permission, from Lenore Walker, "Understanding Battered Woman Syndrome," *Trial*, February 1995.

was about to beat her. After years of abuse, she feared for her unborn child's safety. As the police took her to the homicide division, she was confused. Why were they taking her there, she asked them, when her husband could never die?

Permitting BWS Testimony

I performed a clinical evaluation of Beverly and planned to testify at her murder trial that she was suffering from BWS. The D.C. federal court judge did not admit my testimony, ruling that it was not based on standard medical/psychological evidence. Over the next several years, appellate courts finally set rules permitting testimony on BWS, but it was too late for Beverly, who was convicted of second-degree murder and sentenced to two years in prison.

Today, the testimony has been accepted in courts in every state. Some state legislatures have codified legal decisions about its admissibility, and governors have used it to grant clemency to convicted women serving long sentences. In addition to self-defense cases, the testimony has also proved useful in a variety of situations:

- Criminal courts use it to convict batterers even when the victims are too scared to testify against them.
- The testimony can explain how BWS can be a mitigating factor in cases where women are accused of helping their batterers commit crimes.
- Civil courts permit testimony on BWS to settle possible coercive-contract disputes and to prove liability and damages in domestic tort and other civil cases.
- Family courts hear the testimony to make decisions about the validity of property distribution and child custody and visitation arrangements.
- Wills of battered women have been challenged by using BWS testimony to show that a woman suffering from the syndrome was incompetent when she drew up the document. Even more common, BWS testimony has been used to deny a batterer rights to property when he has killed the woman after a long history of abuse.
- Attorneys representing child abuse victims who kill their abusers use an adapted version to mitigate guilt and to seek lesser sentences.
- Assault victims who have suffered psychological damages also use a modified version of the testimony, as do some sexual harassment victims who bring discrimination cases under Title VII.

What Is Battered Woman Syndrome?

The definition of Battered Woman Syndrome is different in law and psychology, sometimes causing confusion for expert witnesses who are not specially trained in working with abuse victims. The legal system uses BWS to describe both the clinical syndrome and the dynamics of the battering relationship, while mental health professionals use the clinical syndrome to design treatment plans.

Research has shown that many battered women experience a collection of symptoms that have come to be called a syndrome, and mental health providers who testify as experts must incorporate these symptoms into whatever diagnostic system they use. . . .

Experts evaluating victims who might be suffering from BWS look for two major groups of symptoms: (1) the fight-or-flight response and (2) changes in cognitive abilities, judgment, and memory.

Fight or flight. This response has been measured in psychology since the early 1900s. When people are frightened or perceive danger, their autonomic nervous system becomes activated and they enter a state of "hypervigilance" in which the mind and body prepare to deal with the danger. The heart beats faster and breathing changes, other physiological changes occur, and feelings of anxiety increase. The person may become irritable and find it difficult to concentrate. The person may also experience panic attacks if he or she has experienced this danger many times before. This state of high arousal and anxiety constitutes the fight response.

The flight response is characterized by avoidance mechanisms and numbing of emotions. Denial, repression, dissociation, and minimization are the psychological terms that describe unconscious ways of not dealing with what is really occurring. Changes in interpersonal relationships and the belief that the future is short appear during this phase.

Sometimes a person experiences a "seesaw" effect in which the anxiety rises until it gets too high, and then the avoidance and numbing set in. Other times the person experiences these symptoms simultaneously, creating contradictory emotions that seem difficult to explain. Some victims may get stuck in one mode more than the other.

Although battered women are often pictured as passive and unskilled, many have successful careers and can express their angry feelings when they are not afraid they will be harmed. Some even engage in aggressive behaviors toward their abusers and others, taking risks that they might be hurt worse but needing the psychological boost that fighting back or defending themselves or others gives them.

Reexperiencing Past Abuse

Changes in cognitive or thinking abilities, judgment, and memory. Many women reexperience the abuse in their minds either spontaneously, during nightmares, or when they are exposed to familiar stimuli. This might occur, for example, when a person is sitting quietly or watching TV or driving past a place where an abusive incident occurred.

These experiences are so vivid that many women respond as if the abuse were really happening all over again. This reaction will make the perception of danger from subsequent abuse more vivid. The next time the woman believes violence is imminent, especially if she perceives the danger as life threatening, she may go into a dissociative or other mental state and take what she sees as necessary lifesaving actions—including killing the batterer—that she would not take under ordinary circumstances. She will likely do this without thinking through the consequences. Her only goal in this state is to stop the actual or anticipated violent attack.

Sometimes it is difficult for the woman to tell the difference between memories of past abuse and current threats, making her experience of fear and perception of danger even more intense. Memories of abusive incidents may disappear and reappear at different times. Although the mechanism by which this happens is not known, the fact is that sometimes the woman remembers what happened to her and sometimes she does not. Her confused thinking and propensity to go off on tangents when telling a story are ways of keeping the memories of the abuse from being too painful.

In most legal decisions, BWS has been broadened to include descriptions of the dynamics of abuse as well as the psychological impact it has on a victim. Courts may admit testimony about "learned helplessness"—the victim's inability to predict whether what she does will protect herself from further abuse—and about the cycle of violence, which includes a tension-building stage, a battering incident, and a period of loving contrition by the abuser.

With all these elements being discussed, there has been much confusion in the courts about what exactly constitutes the syndrome. When BWS testimony was first introduced, trial courts barred it by challenging its research methodology. This ceased when the American Psychological Association issued an amicus brief supporting the testimony's scientific foundations.

At least one recent commentator has suggested redefining BWS to standardize how the term is used so that psychologists, attorneys, and judges will know what is meant by the testimony. The definition is still evolving, though, so it may be too soon to codify one.

The Dynamics of Abuse

There is no model victim of domestic violence. Abuse occurs across every race, ethnic background, educational level, and socioeconomic group. Despite recent claims in the media that estimates of the extent of violence against women are exaggerated—claims that misrepresent the findings of a few studies—most victims of domestic violence are indeed women and children. Even the elderly who are abused are predominantly women, most of whom are abused by their male partners and sons and not their caretakers, although that is certainly a problem, too.

A report of the American Psychological Association Task Force on

Violence and the Family reviewed the research and cites the power differences between men and women as an important factor in understanding the psychology of abuse. Violence is learned behavior by men, who use it to get what they believe they are entitled to from women. The psychological dynamics are similar in most forms of violence against women and children.

Many people who do not understand the dynamics of domestic violence ask, "Why don't battered women leave?" The answer is that leaving does not stop the violence. Most men who batter are terrified at the thought of separation, and they continue to stalk and harass their victims even after the women leave. In fact, a battered woman's life may be in more danger after she leaves than while living with her abuser.

Special programs to help these men deal with the dysfunctional thinking that propels their obsessive-compulsive behavior are now available. One stabilization program designed for abusive men has a companion program that teaches their partners how to become more empowered.

Factors that Facilitate Violence

Continued violence against women who have left their abusers may be facilitated by child custody and visitation arrangements that expose both mother and child to greater harm. It is not unusual for an abusive man to demand custody of the child as a way to retain power and control over the woman. Although some of these fathers demonstrate acceptable parenting skills, these are the rare cases. More often, these children are continuously exposed to different parenting values, high-conflict situations, and a role model of bully behavior and intimidation that teaches them to take unfair advantage of other people.

When alcohol and other drug abuse are involved, the children often develop serious emotional difficulties that may be expressed through aggressive and violent behavior in the community. Boys exposed to fathers who batter their mothers are 700 times more likely to use violence in their own lives. If a boy was abused himself, it raises the risk factor to 1,000 times that of the boy who did not experience abuse. . . .

Violence against women and children is learned behavior that continues because no one stops it. When battered women or children become frightened and desperate, thinking no one will help them, homicide or suicide—or both—may be the result.

When victims of domestic abuse end up in court, the law and psychology can work together to resolve the complex issues these cases raise. It is true that the psychologist uses inductive methods of scientific inquiry to come to conclusions, and the lawyer uses deductive methods of reasoning to come to sometimes different conclusions. But the intersection of both types of inquiry can help find the truth and contribute to the solution of what is becoming one of society's most pressing problems.

WHY COURTS AWARD BATTERERS CUSTODY

Catherine Elton

According to Catherine Elton, a research reporter for the *New Republic*, men who have been accused or convicted of battering their wives often obtain custody of children during divorce proceedings. Elton examines several reasons why this situation may occur. Abusers are more likely to seek custody than are non-abusers, she points out, and fathers who contest mothers' rights to custody frequently win. Furthermore, Elton maintains that family court judges who are unfamiliar with the nature of domestic violence tend to question the credibility of women who make allegations of abuse. Family court judges favor joint custody and assume that harmonious relations between divorced parents are necessary for the child's welfare, which discourages battered women from making accusations of abuse, Elton explains.

In December 1996, when Judge Nancy Wieben Stock gave O.J. Simpson [who was found liable in February 1997 for the deaths of his ex-wife, Nicole, and Ron Goldman] custody of his children, the nation reacted with shock. Nicole Brown's family, aided by battered women's advocates, not only appealed, but initiated a drive to recall Judge Stock and to pass legislation forbidding judges from placing children with wife-killers.

But Judge Stock's decision, while shocking, was not surprising. It is in fact common for judges to grant fathers who abuse their wives— even fathers convicted of murdering their wives—custody of their children. Says Rita Smith, executive director of the National Coalition Against Domestic Violence, "People don't believe this could be happening, but this happens to people every day." In a 1995 Florida case, for example, a father convicted of murdering his first wife won custody of his kids from a second marriage because their mother was a lesbian.

Abusers Seek Custody More Than Non-Abusers
While there are no national statistics on how many batterers get custody, experts suggest the phenomenon is widespread. Women get cus-

From Catherine Elton, "Father Knows Best," *The New Republic*, March 24, 1997. Reprinted by permission of *The New Republic*. Copyright 1997 by The New Republic Inc.

tody of children far more often than men, about 85 percent of the
time. But one reason for this is that most mothers' requests for custody go uncontested. When fathers do contest, they are at least as
likely to win custody as their ex-wives. In Massachusetts, for instance,
a 1989 state government report showed that contesting fathers won
sole or joint physical custody in 70 percent of cases. Often enough, of
course, fathers who win sole or joint custody do so because there are
compelling arguments against placing the children with the mother.
Nevertheless, men who would seem to have no business raising children—men who have beaten the children's mothers—do often contest custody. Research from the American Psychological Association
shows that husbands who batter their spouses are twice as likely to
seek custody as non-abusive husbands, in part because many abusers
see it as a way to perpetuate control over their ex-wives.

From 1992 to 1997, due to pressure from women's rights activists,
some state legislatures have amended custody laws to acknowledge
that domestic violence has a harmful effect and that this should be
considered in custody decisions. Twenty-seven states have passed legislation requiring judges to consider domestic violence in determining custody. Ten have established a "rebuttable presumption" that it
is not in the best interest of the child to place him or her in the custody of a batterer.

But, even in states where laws require judges to weigh domestic
abuse heavily, they frequently dismiss it, according to a study in *Hofs-
tra Law Review*. One reason is the still pervasive—if remarkable—
belief, vocally articulated by fathers' rights groups, that there is no
necessary connection between violence against wives and violence
against those wives' children. This, despite research by experts such as
Jeff Edleson, professor of social work at the University of Minnesota,
showing that 40 to 60 percent of men who beat their wives also abuse
their children.

Judges Question Women's Credibility

And many judges remain suspicious that allegations of battery are
actually true. Studies show that, even in states with rebuttable presumption provisions, judges often assume wives are making up abuse
charges to gain the upper hand in bitter custody battles. A review of
various such studies by Karen Czapanskiy, a law professor at the University of Maryland, writing in *Family Law Quarterly*, concludes that,
"Credibility accorded to women litigants is less than that accorded to
men litigants. The problem seems particularly acute when the issue is
a woman's accusation that a man has been violent toward her."

Obviously, false charges do occur. But another reason for skepti-
cism is that judges often rely heavily on the recommendations of
court-appointed custody evaluators. And there is no requirement that
these evaluators be trained in the behavioral effects of domestic

abuse, which include apathy, hysteria and anger. To untutored evaluators, such behavior can undermine charges of abuse, rather than support them. As Michéle Harway, research director at California's Phillips Graduate Institute for marriage, family and child counseling, puts it, "The bottom line is that, if the evaluator doesn't have training, he will not be able to see beneath the symptoms and understand where the symptoms come from."

A Conspiracy of Silence

Another factor working against battered women is the widespread assumption of family court judges that harmonious relations between divorced parents are critical to child welfare. Thus, judges increasingly favor joint legal custody arrangements. The joint custody trend—which has its merits, but clearly not when one of the parents is a batterer—has had the unfortunate effect of making battered mothers reluctant to introduce allegations of domestic violence for fear that they will appear inimical to their former husbands. This reluctance augments the natural and well-documented fear of battered women to accuse their tormenters. State laws may inadvertently encourage this conspiracy of silence. In about half the states where judges are required to consider domestic violence as a factor in custody cases, they are also required to consider the "friendliness" of the parents. How "friendly" is a woman who accuses her husband of beating her?

You might think all of this would have feminist activists out in force, battling for binding laws to limit judges' discretion in custody cases involving domestic violence or the murder of a parent. But here the politics get tricky. In the wake of the O.J. civil trial, Republican Assemblywoman Barbara Alby called for legislation in California that would prevent any parent convicted of killing a spouse from winning custody. [AB 200 was made law on October 9, 1997; however, Alby's specific Family Code Section 3044 was not included, maintaining broad court discretion.] Alby found herself facing some unlikely opponents: battered women's advocates. "I get concerned when we make across-the-board judgments and policy. . . . A homicide is not a homicide is not a homicide," said Sue Osthoff, director of the National Clearinghouse for the Defense of Battered Women. Osthoff worries that laws like Alby's that prevent wife-murderers from getting custody could equally be used against women convicted of killing their abusive spouses.

It would be unfair to suggest that women's advocates who oppose Alby's legislation are as responsible for delivering children into the hands of batterers as are the men's rights groups who deny any connection between spousal abuse and child-rearing behavior. The women's advocates have a point in their objection to Alby's bill. And, in any event, this bill would affect the small number of fathers who kill their wives, not the much larger number who simply beat them. Nevertheless, the opposition to Alby's bill in the California legislature and the constant clamoring of fathers' rights groups underscores a disturbing reality. The myth of child custody law is that it exists to protect the interests of the child. But law is shaped by people who are organized and powerful enough to express their interest—by adults: men's advocates and women's advocates and parents who hire their own advocates.

WELFARE REFORM'S EFFECT ON BATTERED WOMEN

Jennifer Gonnerman

In the following selection, Jennifer Gonnerman argues that welfare reform legislation, officially known as The Personal Responsibility and Work Opportunity Reconciliation Act of 1996, does not take into account the situation faced by most battered women. (The act placed time limits on welfare benefits and established work requirements for welfare recipients.) Gonnerman asserts that poverty and the plight of battered women are connected. She maintains that when battered women attempt to better their lives by going to school or starting jobs, their abusers typically attempt to sabotage these efforts. Furthermore, Gonnerman explains, when battered women do find jobs, they have trouble keeping them because they may miss work due to injuries. Often unable to meet the requirements of welfare reform legislation, battered women should be exempt from some of these requirements and should receive special services to help them solve their domestic problems before finding jobs, she concludes. Gonnerman is a journalist and staff writer for the *Village Voice*.

When Bernice Haynes tried to get off welfare by enrolling in a job training program, her boyfriend tossed her textbooks in the trash. He refused to watch their two children while she was in class. And he would pick fights with her when she tried to study.

"Before the final exam, we fought all weekend from Friday to Monday morning," says Haynes, 31, who lives on Chicago's West Side. Haynes never got the chance to open her books over the weekend. "When I went in that Monday, I was exhausted—from the constant verbal abuse, the put-downs, from trying to keep myself alive—that test wasn't on my mind." She flunked. Haynes, who had been attending classes for a year and was trying to become a licensed nurse, was kicked out of the program—just twelve weeks before graduation.

Haynes is one of thousands of domestic violence victims whose abusive partner tried to thwart her efforts to escape poverty. And for

From Jennifer Gonnerman, "Welfare's Domestic Violence," *The Nation*, March 10, 1997. Reprinted with permission of *The Nation* magazine.

women in the same situation, this struggle is about to get much tougher. The most comprehensive study to date—conducted by the Washington State Institute for Public Policy—found that 60 percent of women on Aid to Families with Dependent Children (A.F.D.C.) said they had been physically abused by their boyfriend or spouse at some point. The Better Homes Fund, a Massachusetts nonprofit, recently studied 409 women on A.F.D.C. and found that 63 percent reported being assaulted by their male partner.

Strict Time Limits Hurt Domestic Violence Victims

As the welfare "reform" goes into effect and A.F.D.C. is abolished, domestic violence victims will be among those hardest hit. The new welfare legislation [the Personal Responsibility and Work Opportunity Reconciliation Act of 1996] includes strict time limits governing how quickly recipients must move from welfare to work. But "it's potentially dangerous for domestic violence victims," says Jody Raphael, director of the Chicago-based Taylor Institute, who was one of the first people to study the relationship between household abuse and welfare. "It's predicated on the idea that women become dependent and lazy and really just need a kick in the butt to get out into the labor market. But if you're a past or current domestic violence victim, it'll be exceedingly difficult. Women need support and time to get out of the [abusive] relationship, which they're not going to have under the bill."

The welfare bill's strict time limits range from two months to five years and dictate how long recipients have to find a job, enroll in a training program or start community service before being erased from the welfare rolls. "The rigidity of time limits . . . is not going to be workable," says Martha Davis, legal director of the National Organization for Women (NOW) Legal Defense and Education Fund. It "is likely to result in human tragedy if women are stalked in the workplace but feel they can't change jobs or stop going to work . . . because they'll lose their benefits—or if women in abusive relationships feel they can't leave because there is no safety net for them any longer."

Across the country, activists are fighting to soften the blow of the welfare legislation by urging states to adopt the Family Violence Option as part of their plans. Sponsored by Senators Paul Wellstone of Minnesota and Patty Murray of Washington, this amendment to the 1996 welfare bill urges states to identify victims of battering, refer them to counseling and waive any requirements that unfairly penalize them. As of March 1997, twenty-four of the forty states that have submitted welfare plans adopted part or all of this provision or mentioned domestic violence. "The Family Violence Option is the first time in federal law that the connection between violence and poverty has been recognized," says Davis, who is lobbying hard for it. "Violence makes women poor and it keeps women poor. It's critical that states address that."

Abusers Sabotage Women's Efforts to Work

At first, Bernice Haynes didn't realize her boyfriend of thirteen years was sabotaging her efforts to get off welfare. She recalls justifying the "whuppings" she received by blaming herself. And she remembers how he used to dissuade her from studying. "I was going to give you some money" for dinner, he would say. "But you seem to think that book is more important. Well then, I just suggest you feed those kids with those books." After such a diatribe, Haynes would struggle to "make things right" by acquiescing in her boyfriend's demands and shutting her textbook. Eventually, she woke up to her own abuse and got rid of him. Now she is a case manager at a welfare-to-work program, helping other domestic violence victims make this transition.

From these women, Haynes hears now-familiar tales of boyfriends and husbands undercutting their efforts. "If she makes more money than him, then he doesn't feel like he has power over her. And he doesn't want to lose that power," says Carol Neal, 28, whose boyfriend used to hit her when she started working as a counselor in a Chicago welfare-to-work program.

Domestic violence lawyers, service providers and counselors across the country have collected similar anecdotes. "We see men sabotaging women's efforts both in job training and on the job—men who turn off alarm clocks so the woman oversleeps or who harass [her] through e-mail," says Lucy Friedman, executive director of Victim Services, a New York City nonprofit which used to run a job training program for domestic violence victims. In 1996, the NOW Legal Defense and Education Fund interviewed twenty-five service providers in New York City and found that between 30 and 75 percent of women in their welfare-to-work programs are being abused at home.

Unfortunately, time limits are not the only aspect of the welfare bill that may be especially harmful to battered women. States may now impose a residency requirement, thus penalizing domestic violence victims who flee to another state to insure their safety. And cooperating with the new rule that requires welfare recipients to identify their children's father could put battered women in greater danger.

Proponents of the Family Violence Option are careful to point out that their goal is not to exempt these women permanently from the new work requirements. "We're just trying to provide them with more time and the specific services they need," Raphael says. Ultimately, a job may be exactly what some of these battered women need. "I believe work is often a stronger therapeutic tool than counseling," says Friedman. "It improves their self-esteem and can make them feel in control of their lives."

Determining Eligibility

While the Family Violence Option is supposed to protect domestic violence victims from the changes in welfare, precisely how it will accomplish this remains unclear. The first stumbling block is figuring out which welfare recipients are eligible for waivers. Maria Imperial, who oversaw a job training program for battered women at Victim Services, says, "I don't think many women are going to go into the welfare office and just say, 'I'm a domestic violence victim.'"

One of the first attempts to implement the Family Violence Option is a pilot program on Chicago's West Side, slated to start April 1, 1997. There, workers at the public aid office won't wait for women to announce that they're victims of domestic violence. Instead, the staff will tell female recipients that they may be excused from going to work within two years if it will put them in greater danger of abuse at home.

To find out about past and current abuse, the workers will ask four questions. The first inquires whether "someone in your life with whom you have or had a relationship" has engaged in "pushing, grabbing, shoving, slapping, hitting, restraining," among other abuses. If the woman answers yes, she is sent to a domestic violence counselor and may be exempted from some of the new welfare requirements.

Criticism of this program has yet to mount, although it is not difficult to imagine detractors insisting that some women will lie about being abused in order to stay on the welfare rolls. A more immediate hurdle, however, may be the general lack of awareness about domestic violence. While it is possible for states to waive welfare's time limits, it is not possible to legislate sensitivity.

Meanwhile, experts warn that if states do not attempt to tackle domestic violence from the outset by granting waivers to those who need them, their welfare-to-work programs will fail. Martha Baker, the executive director of Nontraditional Employment for Women, learned this lesson firsthand. Her Manhattan-based program trains women on welfare to work in plumbing, construction and other blue-collar jobs. Baker estimates that 50 percent of her clients are being abused at home—and she encourages them to confront this issue before joining the work force. Otherwise, she says, the problem "rears its ugly head. And once it does, the women are in danger of losing their jobs because they're not showing up, or they come in looking like they've had the stuffing beat out of them, or they have some guy coming around who looks like a stalker."

INSURANCE DISCRIMINATION AGAINST BATTERED WOMEN

Deborah L. Shelton

Deborah L. Shelton is a Chicago-based writer who specializes in medical issues. According to Shelton, some insurance companies have denied medical coverage to women who are victims of domestic abuse. These insurers consider domestic abuse to be a pre-existing medical condition and therefore refuse coverage to women whose medical records show evidence of abuse, Shelton writes. However, she maintains, denying insurance coverage to battered women sends the wrong message to both these women and their physicians. For example, she points out, battered women need to report abuse to their physicians in order to have evidence for any later legal action they may take against their abuser, but they may be reluctant to do so to avoid being denied insurance coverage. Physicians are often mandated to report abuse, but they may decline to do so if they have reason to believe the patient's insurance claim will be rejected, Shelton adds. However, the American Medical Association, the American Bar Association, and advocates for battered women are working to prohibit insurance discrimination against victims of domestic violence, the author explains.

The last thing the 25-year-old Pennsylvania woman expected was to be victimized by insurance companies for being a victim.

But that's exactly what happened when she sought medical care after her husband shoved her into some furniture during an argument, injuring one of her hips.

Medical Records Reveal Abuse

Two national companies later cited the single episode of abuse in denying her applications for insurance: health coverage, in one case, and health, life and disability coverage, in the other. They learned of the woman's injury through a routine review of her medical records.

Ironically, she had been encouraged by a battered women's group

From Deborah L. Shelton, "Twice a Victim," *Human Rights*, Winter 1996. Copyright ©1996 by the American Bar Association. Reprinted by permission.

to have the injury documented in her record in case she later needed to seek a court order of protection. To ensure that injuries caused by family violence are documented, legal advocates, womens' groups and others have waged a vigorous campaign in recent years to encourage battered spouses to share information with their doctors about abuse they've experienced.

As it turns out, her experience of being denied insurance coverage because she'd been injured by her husband wasn't unique.

A survey in 1996 by U.S. Rep. Charles Schumer (D-NY) found that eight of 16 of the largest insurers in his state used domestic abuse as an underwriting criteria.

And a March 1996 survey of life, health, and accident insurers in Pennsylvania by state insurance commissioner Linda S. Kaiser found that 28 percent of 437 companies used domestic violence to decide whether to provide coverage. Among health insurers, 22 percent said they would consider domestic abuse in deciding whether to cover an individual. And 8 percent of health insurers said they would take a history of abuse into account when deciding whether to renew a policy.

"A Pre-Existing Medical Condition"

"Insurance companies, it appears, have refused to cover victims of domestic violence—as one company representative said in 1995, on the grounds that covering battered women is like 'covering diabetics who refused to take their insulin,'" U.S. Rep. Constance A. Morella (D-MD) told a Senate committee hearing on insurance discrimination in July 1996. "Domestic violence has now become a pre-existing medical condition."

Richard Coorsh, spokesman for the Health Insurance Assn. of America, which represents many of the nation's private health insurance carriers, said his group's members do not target victims of abuse, but that underwriting does take place. "Virtually all carriers that issue individual coverage must underwrite for that coverage and the person's entire history is taken into account," Coorsh said. "Because of the nature of the individual market, underwriting is necessary." He added that avoiding high-risk applicants keeps rates reasonable for everyone.

What has alarmed many womens' advocates is that, as in the case of the Pennsylvania woman, a history of abuse often comes to an insurer's attention, not through information provided by the applicant, but through an underwriter's review of patient medical records.

After she was rejected for life insurance in 1994, a 31-year-old Delaware woman learned that she had been turned down because of "confidential medical information." She later learned that an off-the-record discussion she had with her doctor in January 1990 about her depressed husband's history of addiction had made it into her medical record. She also found out that three incidents involving injuries caused by her husband had also been recorded. The company said the incidents indicated "an unstable family environment."

"There are some real ethical issues," said the woman's attorney, Jan R. Jurden, who works on a volunteer basis with the Domestic Violence Coordinating Council in Delaware. "Where do you draw the line? What obligation is the doctor under to comply with the insurance company's request? And what obligation does the doctor have to the patient to screen information before it's made available to the insurance company?"

The Number of Victimized Women Is Unknown

It's not clear how many women have been denied insurance or had claims rejected or rates raised because they had been battered. "We know that a lot of people are being victimized by domestic violence, so we can conclude that this is happening to a lot of people," said Terry Fromson, staff attorney with the Women's Law Project in Philadelphia, who with the Pennsylvania Coalition Against Domestic Violence provided the woman with legal assistance.

"Furthermore, without documentation of their suffering they will be impeded in their efforts to obtain civil and criminal remedies that can prevent their injury and death."

American Bar Association (ABA) policy urges adoption of legislation at the state and federal level that would ensure that an applicant cannot be denied insurance benefits solely on the basis of the individual's status as a victim of domestic violence.

"We don't hold victims of crime responsible for their injuries," said ABA president Roberta Cooper Ramo when the policy was adopted. "Insurance companies do not deny coverage for an individual who has been shot or stabbed by a stranger. They should not revoke coverage when the attacker is a spouse."

Family violence is a public health problem that crosses boundaries of age, class, or race. Yet many women, out of feelings of helplessness, shame, or embarrassment, don't seek help. A 1994 survey by Louis Harris and Associates, conducted for the Commonwealth Fund, a national philanthropy based in New York City, estimated that 3.9 million, or 7 percent, of all women living with a spouse or partner had been abused. Of those women, 92 percent had never discussed the abuse with their physicians.

In recent years, health care organizations and patient-advocacy groups have pushed for protocols to better identify and treat victims of family violence and ensure they are referred to appropriate medical and social services. The federal government's "Healthy People 2000" initiative set as a goal that by the end of the decade health care professionals should respond adequately to at least 90 percent of such patients who present at hospital emergency departments.

"The American Medical Association (AMA) has strived to facilitate the reporting and diagnosis of domestic abuse in an effort to identify and help the problem before it goes too far," American Medical Association trustee Dr. Timothy T. Flaherty told the Senate Committee on Labor and Human Resources on July 28, 1996. "Recent insurance company practices threaten to impede our valuable progress in this area."

In 1995, the AMA House of Delegates condemned the practice of denying insurance coverage to victims of domestic violence and called on the association to seek federal legislation to prohibit such discrimination.

Protective Legislation

Since then, bills have been introduced in both houses of Congress. The AMA supports a measure proposed by U.S. Sen. Paul Wellstone (D-MN), which would prohibit insurers from denying health insurance coverage or benefits or increasing premiums solely because the applicant had been abused. It also would prohibit classifying injuries resulting from abuse as a pre-existing condition.

"Right now battered women are being put into this horrible position of being battered again," Wellstone said. "Because then what happens is that they see the insurance policy canceled or the rates set at such an exorbitant rate that they can't afford it. It's the worst possible example of blaming the victim."

Another bill, introduced in the House, would require states to enact laws prohibiting the discrimination or face a $10,000-a-day fine. It also would prohibit employer health plans from changing or eliminating coverage to victims of domestic violence.

Legislation and regulations addressing the issue also have been proposed in 14 states, five of which have enacted measures.

Most of the state bills mirror legislation drafted by the National Assn. of Insurance Commissioners (NAIC), an organization of state insurance regulators. Its model bill would prohibit the use of abuse status, abuse-related conditions, and a history of abuse-related claims as a basis for insurance coverage and claims settlement decisions.

The model legislation includes a section prohibiting insurers from breaching the confidentiality of an abuse victim's medical, police, court, credit, employment, or insurance records unless the victim specifically authorizes access to those records. It also requires insurers to disclose their reasons for unfavorable claims or coverage decisions.

Until the issue is addressed legislatively, patients should refuse to sign a blanket release form that makes all information in the records available to insurers evaluating their eligibility, said AMA trustee Dr. Robert E. McAfee, chair of the National Advisory Council on Family Violence.

He urged physicians to continue asking patients about suspected abuse. "We don't want to dissuade colleagues from being better evidence technicians in documenting the facts of the case in a way that will be helpful down the road."

Some advocates for battered women have suggested that physicians separate abuse information from the rest of a patient's medical record. But Dr. Wanda Filer, who chairs the medical advisory task force of the Pennsylvania Coalition Against Domestic Violence, disagrees. "It's a disincentive to start asking the questions. We are trying to break down barriers; we don't need [to erect] another one. What would happen is that [providers] would say, 'Forget it, I'm not going to ask.'"

In fact, physicians who fail to document evidence of domestic violence may be breaking the law in states that mandate physician reporting, said Roberta Valente, staff director of the ABA's Commission on Domestic Violence. Forty states have mandatory physician reporting requirements that apply in at least some instances of family violence.

Insurers Review Old Procedures

The Pennsylvania woman, whose 1993 case first shed light on the problem, has since obtained health and life insurance from one of the companies that turned her down, State Farm Insurance Cos., based in Bloomington, Ill. State Farm, the nation's sixth largest life insurer and third largest individual health insurer, announced in 1996 that it would no longer use evidence of domestic violence to determine eligibility of an applicant, said spokeswoman K. C. Eynatten.

"It was nothing we had ever asked ourselves about," she said. "If we were in effect keeping victims from moving out of the house, that was the last thing we wanted to do. Domestic violence is no longer used in any way in the underwriting procedure. We don't ask the question, and if the information comes up, it's not used. It's not part of the process at all."

First Colony Life Insurance Co., based in Lynchburg, Va., was the other company that refused the Pennsylvania woman coverage. Citing confidentiality, vice president David H. McMahon declined to talk about the case, but he said the company was "participating with the American Council of Life Insurance and the [NAIC] to try to come up with model legislation that will address this industry-wide problem and meet the needs of the public and insurers."

The Delaware woman, who has not been identified publicly, was eventually offered life insurance from the company that had initially rejected her, but she declined and has since purchased insurance elsewhere.

Since the Pennsylvania and Delaware cases have come to light, other women have reported similar experiences. For example, a California woman said she was repeatedly turned down for health insurance following a review of medical records that detailed beatings she received from her husband, according to U.S. Sen. Nancy L. Kassebaum (R-KS), who testified on the issue at the July 1996 Senate hearing.

When Wellstone introduced his legislation in March 1996, he described the plight of a woman who had sought help from a St. Cloud, Minn., shelter. She was hospitalized with a broken jaw and spent two weeks in a psychiatric unit. Two insurance companies later denied her coverage.

Nancy Durborow, health projects coordinator for the Pennsylvania Coalition Against Domestic Violence, said denial of benefits cuts victims off from medical care and discourages them from seeking help. "Not being able to obtain health, automobile, or homeowner's insurance because of domestic violence means a mother can't afford to take her kids to the doctor, can't provide for her kids in the event of her disability or death, can't own a car, or own or even rent a home— all critical factors in establishing a life free of violence."

Prior to the highly publicized Pennsylvania case, domestic violence advocates were unaware of insurance discrimination against victims of abuse, primarily because insurers are not required to disclose the reasons for denial of insurance.

"It was only due to the persistence of this young woman in demanding that the insurance companies provide her with a reason for the denial that we were tipped off to this longstanding practice," Durborow said.

Said Deborah Senn, chair of the NAIC panel that developed the model state legislation: "What's so highly disturbing about these cases is that they send absolutely the wrong message to people: that if you talk to your doctor, if you talk to police, you'll be victimized economically."

CHAPTER 4

PERSONAL STORIES OF ABUSE AND SURVIVAL

Contemporary Issues
Companion

THE WOMAN WHO CANNOT STOP CRYING

Tamara Jones

In November 1987, Joel Steinberg and his common-law wife, Hedda Nussbaum, were arrested for the beating death of their illegally adopted six-year-old daughter, Lisa. Examination of Nussbaum by physicians and psychiatrists revealed that for twelve years she had been severely abused physically and mentally by Steinberg. Nussbaum was never indicted by the prosecutor, who determined that she could not be held accountable for Lisa's death. Many Americans, however, blamed Nussbaum for failing to protect Lisa from Steinberg's abuse. In the following selection, Tamara Jones, a staff writer for the *Washington Post*, interviews Nussbaum ten years after Lisa's death. Jones recounts the life of torture and abuse that Nussbaum experienced with Steinberg and describes the lasting effects of this abuse on Nussbaum's life.

The cottage sits on a wooded knoll, tucked well away from view. A woman with a shy, crooked smile answers the door. There is something hauntingly familiar about her face, framed now by wiry dark hair going gray. You know her, but you don't. It is a Picasso face, compelling yet somehow disturbing, the features not quite aligned. "I'm Hedda," she says simply.

A Symbol of Domestic Violence

After her arrest in November 1987, Hedda Nussbaum became a household name, both reviled and pitied as she took the witness stand in a nationally televised murder trial and implicated her lover, Joel Steinberg, in the beating death of their illegally adopted 6-year-old daughter, Lisa. With her shattered face and her detached demeanor, Nussbaum became a symbol of domestic violence and America's conflicted feelings about battered women. Back then, in rote, zombielike tones, she told a New York City courtroom how Steinberg tortured and beat her for years, how he turned his rage one night on little Lisa—leaving her crumpled on the bathroom floor—and how she, Nussbaum, failed

Reprinted from Tamara Jones, "The Woman Who Can't Stop Crying," *Good Housekeeping*, June 1997, by permission of the author.

to get help until it was too late.

Today, watching in fascination as woodpeckers build a nest outside her kitchen window, she seems almost serene. After spending years in virtual seclusion and undergoing intensive psychiatric treatment, she has decided to put herself back in the public eye. In March 1997, a New York court opened the door for her to seek civil damages from Steinberg, extending the one-year statute of limitations for cases involving domestic violence. When the decision was announced, Nussbaum, now 55, confidently appeared before the TV cameras, reading a statement about the significance of the ruling for all battered women. That was the beginning. Now there are matters she wants to resolve, a reputation she hopes to rebuild, and a world she longs to rejoin beyond the walls of this tiny rented home in upstate New York.

Spare but tidy, the one-bedroom cottage is a far cry from the cluttered and filthy apartment she once shared with Steinberg, an attorney, in Manhattan's fashionable Greenwich Village. The walls here are decorated with framed photographs Nussbaum has taken of tranquil landscapes, and the kitchen cupboards are full of the mugs and bowls she made in art therapy. This is her sanctuary. Yet the overall effect is more dreary than cozy. The muddy earthtones of her pottery, the shadows dominating her photographs, even the shower curtain and towels hanging in the bathroom are deep brown. It is as if, unable to escape the darkness, she has embraced it.

In the cramped living room, a rocking chair rests against a wall. "I used to rock my babies in that chair and sing to them," Nussbaum remarks almost idly. "I had a beautiful singing voice." The voice is husky now, her vocal cords permanently damaged from Steinberg's throttlings.

Steinberg had taken first Lisa and later another newborn, Mitchell, from unwed mothers, telling them he was an adoption lawyer who would legally place their babies for a fee. After Nussbaum and Steinberg were arrested in November 1987, 16-month-old Mitchell was returned to his natural mother, and Nussbaum never saw him again.

Nussbaum's Trauma Still Raises Questions

When Hedda Nussbaum's name is mentioned, the response almost invariably is a surprised question: Is she out now? But Nussbaum was never indicted in connection with Lisa's death. The prosecutor determined she could not be held accountable because of her physical and mental condition. Still, as a traumatized woman who could not—or would not—save her child, she never fit neatly into the category of pure victim. And the tough questions asked a decade ago cannot help but resurface now. She and Steinberg were together for 12 hellish years. Why didn't she leave him? Why didn't she seek help? Nussbaum is still struggling for answers, but she is willing to make herself vulnerable again.

Specifically, she wants to reach out to other battered women, to give them the courage and support she never had. She wants to comfort their children. "I think I can really help," she says, her flat voice suddenly dropping to a near-whisper. "Otherwise, what's the point of my being alive?"

That she is still alive is testament to her deep, primal instinct for survival. At the time of her arrest, Nussbaum was a half-starved, crippled recluse. Her legs had gangrenous, ulcerous wounds where Steinberg had beaten her with a stick, and doctors at the hospital where police took her in handcuffs said that without treatment, she would have died of blood poisoning within a matter of days. Her lip was swollen and split, her eye blackened, her ear cauliflowered like a boxer's from repeated blows, her nose collapsed from all the times it had been broken. Several teeth were missing. Her cheekbones had been smashed, her knee fractured, her spleen ruptured, her jaw splintered, and 16 ribs cracked at one time or another. More difficult to assess was the emotional damage. Attorney Betty Levinson, who represents Nussbaum and has befriended her, remembers being shocked when she first saw her new client. "Never, ever in my life had I seen a human being in such condition. She was utterly pathetic, utterly forlorn, utterly confused, and totally enraptured with Joel Steinberg."

Psychiatrists who examined Nussbaum would liken her to a hostage or a prisoner of war, robbed of her free will and grasp of reality by a tormentor whose approval had come to mean everything to her. A former schoolteacher and children's book editor who had been known for her lively, inquisitive mind, Nussbaum was consumed by Steinberg, even after her arrest. Even as Lisa lay comatose in the hospital with brain injuries. And even though Mitchell had been whisked away by the police that November morning. Her own fate didn't interest her either. "I only wanted to know about Joel," she admits now. "Was Joel all right?"

The Long Road to Recovery

Nussbaum spent 13 months in a private psychiatric facility before she was able to function again. One sleepless night, she got up and began sketching in the journal doctors insisted she keep. She copied a picture of Steinberg from a newspaper clipping. Suddenly she was filled with a white-hot rage. "Look what you did to me!" she wrote. "And all in front of our child. . . . She had to be secretly terrified. She had to see her life turning into what mine was. Beatings upon beatings. Bruises, blood, horror. My poor baby. Why didn't I see it? Why didn't I stop it?"

Sobbing, she began a new page. "Lisa, Lisa," she wrote. I'm sorry. God forgive me. I'm sorry." She made a promise to her dead daughter: "It's too late to see now, Lisa. But maybe we can help others. Maybe we can save another child's life. That's not enough for us. But it's all we have, Lisa."

Sitting now at a dining-room table she once shared with Steinberg, Nussbaum describes what happened with almost clinical detachment, pausing occasionally to search for a precise word—the lingering effect, she believes, of slight brain damage caused by Steinberg's blows. She sips herbal tea and wears a thin red sweater over her shoulders. She frets about her waistline—"I can't run because he broke my knee"— and wonders whether further plastic surgery might someday give her a more normal-looking nose. But her story is told without fury or bitterness. Others call Steinberg a monster; Nussbaum does not. It's as though she occupies an emotional safety zone, her truest self cordoned off and untouchable, a crime scene surrounded by yellow police tape. Bessel van der Kolk, M.D., a prominent psychiatrist who examined her in 1994, concluded that the full terror of what happened in Apartment 3W has never fully penetrated. "If it does," he wrote in his report, "her depression is likely to become disabling."

Even with Steinberg locked away in prison (he was convicted of first-degree manslaughter), she remains sheltered from the real world. Her friends come mainly from the protective network of advocates for battered women. Neither Levinson nor the psychiatrist Nussbaum still sees, Samuel Klagsbrun, has ever sent her a bill. She is recognized in her small town but mostly left in peace. There have been a few incidents, though: A stranger shouted "Murderer!" at her in the supermarket, and a passing motorist called her a child abuser. A local women's art gallery agreed to display some of her nature photographs but canceled the exhibit after receiving bomb threats. Still, Nussbaum insists that much of the attention she attracts is positive, that strangers wish her well, and that the abused women she counsels find her "inspirational" because she survived.

For years, Nussbaum tried to get back into the publishing world, but found herself frozen out. The one editorial job offer she got was rescinded "because the staff apparently objected."

She retrained as a word processor and a legal secretary. Still, no one wanted her on the payroll, and she lived for a number of years on unemployment and temp work. In 1993, she was finally hired as a full-time legal secretary, but the job ended when her boss died. Recently, she landed another job. "I like it a lot," she says. "The people are very, very nice." She is grateful for the compliments she gets on the letters she types. Her work is valued, and no one in the law firm asks her about the past.

Recalling Nussbaum's Past with Steinberg

Her publishing career was just getting off the ground when she met Steinberg at a party in 1975. Nussbaum was 33 years old, the shy, younger daughter of an immigrant Polish hairdresser and his homemaker wife. Her only sibling, an older sister named Judy, had married and was raising a son in New Jersey. Nussbaum yearned for the same kind of life. She'd had boyfriends, had even followed one out to California, but none was ready to commit to her.

Steinberg, a well-to-do attorney who boasted of mob connections and a past in military espionage, was as brash as Nussbaum was tentative. "He was very, very charming," she recalls now. "Very bright. He just seemed terrific in every way." After dating for a few weeks, Nussbaum felt smothered by Steinberg's constant demands on her time and broke it off. But the romance was rekindled several months later, and before long, Nussbaum had moved into his apartment. Steinberg made her his project, giving her "assignments" for self-improvement. Ask a merchant for change without buying anything. Ask for a raise. "It really worked." Nussbaum still marvels. "I started becoming much more outgoing, and I gave him credit for every improvement." When Steinberg complained that she lacked the grace of his previous girlfriend, Nussbaum took ballet lessons. She felt herself falling deeper in love with her Svengali, brushing aside the concerns of friends. Steinberg began pointing out their "flaws" to Nussbaum—this one wasn't "classy" enough, that one was too selfish—and ever so slowly, she shut them out. Her parents and sister began keeping their distance too. Steinberg made them feel unwelcome at the apartment, and usually claimed Nussbaum was busy or gone when they called.

One day after they had been living together for three years, Steinberg grabbed her by the collar and angrily slammed her up against the stove. His words became a chilling prophecy. "He said he could be dangerous sometimes," Nussbaum says. Not long after that, she ended up in the emergency room for the first time after Steinberg punched her in the eye so hard she was seeing flashing lights. "Oh, this is just something that happened," Nussbaum assured a sympathetic stranger sitting next to her in the hospital waiting room. "This incident brought us closer together." Unlike many batterers, Steinberg did not express remorse after beating his lover, nor did he shower her with gifts. "It was like one second of anger . . . then we were close again," Nussbaum says.

The beatings became more frequent. Steinberg always insisted they were for her own good, to help her "reach a better place" mentally. Showing up at work with bruises and black eyes, Nussbaum would invent stories about having been mugged or falling down. Steinberg would rehearse her lies with her before she left the apartment. When he ruptured her spleen, she told her family that she had an infection. Yet even in the face of the escalating violence, Nussbaum clung to her fantasy that she and Steinberg were deeply in love and everything would be all right. She even wrote a children's book, *Plants Do Amazing Things*, and dedicated it to Steinberg, "my everyday inspiration."

"He had helped me so much, he had given me so much," she says now. "I loved him so much. I separated the Joel I loved, the good Joel, from the bad Joel, whom I saw only briefly."

The Decision to Adopt

After trying without success to conceive a child, the couple decided to adopt. A colleague came into Nussbaum's office one day and shut the door. "How are you going to protect this child when you can't protect yourself?" the coworker demanded. Nussbaum remembers feeling outraged: *How dare she!* The denial still echoes, disturbingly, today. "Joel," she asserts, "did have a wonderful relationship with Lisa. He was very good to her, gave her a lot of attention. I thought he was a terrific father."

Lisa was only a day old when Steinberg brought her home. "I was so happy," Nussbaum recalls. "I finally had my baby that I wanted so bad. She was a good baby. She didn't cry a lot." The beatings stopped for several months, and Steinberg even talked of buying a luxury penthouse for his new family. When the violence flared again, though, it was worse than before. Nussbaum missed so much work and became so unreliable that she was fired. Steinberg had her stay home and work without pay as his legal secretary. He worked from bed, getting up only to go out to dinner with increasingly low-life clients, mostly drug dealers. One of them taught them how to make rock cocaine, and they would freebase while Lisa slept—a practice that, even now, Nussbaum dismisses as merely "being naughty."

Sometimes she remembers, after pummeling her, Steinberg would "heal" her by rubbing his hands over the bruises or putting her in an icy bath to reduce the swelling. Once he realized how much she hated the freezing baths, they became a new form of torture. As Nussbaum sat in the tub watching her fingernails turn blue, Steinberg would come in periodically to check on her "to see if I was in the right place yet."

Naomi Weiss, one of Nussbaum's old college friends who had drifted away, remembers feeling stunned when she saw Nussbaum's battered picture in the newspapers the day after her arrest. "Nobody helped her. Nobody read the messages right," Weiss laments. She has resumed the friendship, watching Nussbaum "come through an enormous amount of pain and struggling and suffering." They chat on the phone occasionally, and go out for dinner in New York City. Though Weiss has seen strangers on the street come up to Nussbaum and say, "God bless you," members of Weiss's own family have shunned her because of the association. The urge to hate Nussbaum is as strong as the urge to save her.

Nussbaum doesn't really blame anyone—apart from Steinberg—for her years of torment. Still, no one seems to have tried very hard to intervene. Not the neighbors who called police to complain about the noise of people fighting in Apartment 3W. Not the officers who came to the door and took Steinberg's word that everything was fine. Not the social workers who twice responded to reports of child neglect but failed to follow up, or the teachers who noticed Lisa's bruises but accepted her explanations that her baby brother had hit her.

Half-Hearted Attempts to Leave

"I tried to leave Joel five and a half times," Nussbaum says. She would make it to the airport or a hospital or the doorstep of some acquaintance, then immediately call him and go back home again. Once, she didn't even make it out the door. She never told anyone what was happening, not even her parents or her beloved sister. "Nobody could have rescued me," she insists. "I wouldn't have wanted them to rescue me."

At a birthday party for her sister not long ago, Nussbaum offered a toast, telling partygoers how much she loved Judy, and repeating an oft-told family story: When the newborn Hedda was brought home, her sister had said "my baby." Judy had always taken care of her and protected her when they were children, Nussbaum recalled. Judy began to sob. "Why are you crying?" Nussbaum asked in dismay. "Because I really didn't protect you," her sister responded.

Now, when she counsels battered women, Nussbaum urges them to do what she never did: have a plan, decide where to go. "They should save money, pack clothes, hide things they need, get copies of documents," she says. One night, a woman attending the support group for the first time said something about her husband leaving bruises on her daughter's arms. Nussbaum felt a chill as she listened. "I said to her, 'I don't want to scare you, but your daughter could end up like mine.' Of course, I did want to scare her. She got her husband out. She says she owes that to me."

Nussbaum never seriously tried to get Steinberg out of her life. By November 1987, he had grown more and more paranoid, accusing Nussbaum of trying to hypnotize him and the children, and lure them into a nonexistent cult. He jabbed at Nussbaum's dark brown eyes, once ripping a tear duct. He made her sleep on the floor, naked and without a blanket, and wouldn't let her eat anything except food she foraged at night from supermarket Dumpsters. She wasted away to less than 100 pounds. Nussbaum now believes that some of Steinberg's bizarre behavior was the result of cocaine-induced psychosis. But she does not regard him as insane. "Battering is not a mental illness," she points out. "It's a choice. He didn't beat up clients in his office. He didn't call the guy at the store names or punch him in the nose. He did that to me."

Because of a pending lawsuit filed by Lisa's biological mother, Nussbaum refuses to go into detail about the events leading up to Lisa's fatal injuries, except to say that Steinberg was forcing them both to eat hot peppers that day because he thought they weren't drinking enough water. He and Lisa were in the bathroom. Then Lisa was unconscious on the floor, struggling to breathe. Nussbaum believed Steinberg had poured water into her nose and throat: "I thought she was drowning."

Suddenly, Nussbaum leaves the safety zone, and the pain seems to overwhelm her. "I'm someone who loved Lisa and never meant her any harm," she cries. "I really did everything I possibly could at that moment, from where I was coming from, to try and save her. I was giving her artificial respiration. Joel was coming over and showing me the correct way to do it." He left to go out to dinner. *Don't worry,* he told Nussbaum, *when I come home, I'll get her up.* Nussbaum claims she genuinely believed he could heal Lisa, "and that's why I didn't call for help, even though I thought of it." Summoning help, she reasoned, would also be disloyal to Steinberg. She must never be disloyal.

He returned three hours later, and eventually agreed to let her dial 911. Steinberg went with the ambulance, then came home and said he was worried Lisa might be brain-damaged because she had gone without oxygen for too long. The blame, he implied, was hers.

And yet, Nussbaum remembers that morning as one not of grief or panic, but tenderness. Steinberg pulled her onto the bed and they cuddled. When the police came to arrest them, it went without saying that Nussbaum would lie for him. She was taken to the hospital, where her own injuries were videotaped. She had wrapped paper towels around the ulcerated wounds on her legs because there were no bandages in the house.

The press accounts describing the children as dirty and the apartment as a dark, filthy cave still upset Nussbaum, especially the report that police found Mitchell drinking sour milk. "I would never, ever feed my children spoiled milk!" she cries now. "That was fresh milk from the refrigerator."

Mourning Lisa

"I think I was a good mother because I loved my kids," she reflects. "I gave them lots of care and attention and love." When she was at the mental hospital, she felt the need to say good-bye. A psychodrama was staged, and an anorexic patient assumed the role of Lisa, with Nussbaum supplying the dialogue. She went to hug Lisa and began to cry for the first time since her arrest. "I talked to her," Nussbaum recalls. "She said, 'Don't cry, Mommy, I'm okay.'" Nussbaum fails to see the irony here—the first time she was able to give voice to the child she left dying on the bathroom floor, Lisa was comforting *her*.

Nussbaum visits Lisa's grave from time to time, leaving little plastic toys that won't be ruined in the rain. She keeps a lock of Lisa's chestnut hair and framed photographs of Lisa and Mitchell, whose natural mother settled a civil suit against Nussbaum, the terms of which are sealed. After Lisa's death, Nussbaum found a pen pal overseas: a 10-year-old girl. When the girl turned 13, Nussbaum told her what had happened.

"My husband used to hit me," she wrote, "and then suddenly he hit our daughter when she was six years old, and she died. He's in prison now and will be for a very long time. Nobody has the right to hit anybody else, don't you agree?" The young pen pal and her family expressed their sorrow, and stayed in touch.

Nussbaum says she has had no contact with Steinberg since the trial, and though she longs to have a healthy, enduring relationship with another man, "I haven't met anyone yet." She dabbles in photography and writing, and watches the birds she has taught herself to recognize from an ornithology book. The woodpeckers weren't building a nest after all, she complains, "just sharpening their beaks." She is working on a new book for children, a question-and-answer guide titled *Why Does Dad Hit Mom?*, but she doubts anyone will publish it because of her notoriety. "I hope now you've read this, you can understand you're not alone," the book concludes.

Hedda Nussbaum is alone. She is trying to grow begonias, but the leggy plant in her cottage window seems hungry for more light. She never has nightmares; she stopped dreaming altogether when she was with Steinberg. The doctors have patched her together as best as they can. But they were never able to fix the torn tear duct, and her left eye waters indiscriminately. She cannot stop weeping. Steinberg has never publicly admitted guilt, never expressed remorse. He will be in prison, if not paroled, for at least another six years. And Hedda Nussbaum remains free to sleep through dreamless nights and sing her silent lullabies and try through the ceaseless tears to reach, someday, a better place.

Is Leaving Better?

Stephanie Rodriguez

Stephanie Rodriguez is a formerly battered woman and the author of *Time to Stop Pretending*, an autobiographical account of her experience with domestic violence from her childhood with an abusive father to her escape from an abusive husband. In the following selection, she illustrates why many battered women find it difficult to leave their abusers. When she left her abuser, Rodriguez explains, she not only faced the threat of poverty and homelessness, but also ridicule and harassment as a single mother. When women with children leave abusive relationships, she argues, they become single mothers, and many Americans believe that single mothers are destructive to society. Authorities and neighbors have little compassion for the struggles facing single mothers trying to escape abuse, which makes it difficult for these women to leave abusive relationships, Rodriguez concludes.

Yet another woman was killed by her estranged husband in Indianapolis, and yet again the question was asked, "Why don't these battered women leave?" Well, they do. She left and she paid the ultimate price for daring to do so. Statistics gathered by the National Coalition Against Domestic Violence tell us that this woman wasn't unusual, that women who leave their batterer are at a 75% greater risk of being murdered than are women who stay. Battered women leave all the time and are punished for it. Those who are not killed for their insolence are often so severely punished by society that they quickly go back or jump into another equally abusive partnership.

Becoming a Single Mother

We do leave and the majority of us have children and we get assigned a new role. We transform, as if by magic, from wives and mothers (pillars of our civilization) into horrid society-murdering beasts. We become SINGLE MOTHERS.

I made that change some time ago. A fear for my life and for the lives of my children pushed me to abandon everything I had and to move hundreds of miles from the only home my children had ever

Reprinted, with permission, from Stephanie Rodriguez, "Is Leaving Better?" *Family Violence Pages*, 1995, @ http://www.famvi.com/leave.htm.

known. Believe me, I had cause to re-think that decision many times over the first few years. Not only did I become a single mother when I left, but my family became an entirely different kind of family, somehow less valuable without a man. Less valuable and a lot more vulnerable. Let me tell you about one night in particular.

We'd been here for about four years the night that my neighbors sent a representative to knock on my door. We were sitting on the dining room floor (just till we got a dining room table, mind you), eating our bologna sandwiches (it was always bologna sandwiches when the gas was cut off), not feeling too sorry for ourselves about the gas (at least it was summer, we weren't freezing), when there came a knock on the door. I peeped cautiously out from the sheet on the window to make sure it wasn't some welfare worker or anybody else likely to make trouble about what we didn't have. Satisfied that it was a neighbor of mine, I opened the door. She didn't waste any time, this neighbor of mine, but told me quickly and clearly why she had come. Some of the neighbors had gotten together it seemed, and they'd decided that they would like for me to move, and as quickly as possible if I didn't mind. Just like that—please move. I stared for a moment wondering if they could do that—ask me to move—I didn't know. The problem? The crime I'd committed that merited throwing me out of the neighborhood? I hadn't mowed my grass, and it was beginning to look really bad on the whole neighborhood, she said.

A Pointing Finger, Not a Helping Hand

Now, after four years on our own, it still took every penny I could get my hands on to pay my rent and feed my children. We still didn't have beds to sleep in or furniture to sit on, we had no money and no utilities, but these neighbors hadn't come to me with the offer of loaning me a lawn mower, No. There had been no helping hand at the end of their outstretched arm, only a pointing finger. Was I insensitive to the needs of my community? Perhaps, but on top of everything else, I just couldn't see how I could manage to get a lawn mower. We moved. And as quickly as possible.

That was quite a while ago, but things like that are still going on. Just this year [1995] I saw my landlord evict the woman from the house next to mine (also an escaped battered woman, also with small children) for the offense of having her utilities disconnected for nonpayment.

These are the types of treatment that crush the strength a woman has mustered to get out of an abusive situation. Her strength alone can only take her so far. After that she needs the help of others. It doesn't have to be money. It could be something as simple as the loan of a lawn mower. Maybe some compassion, a little understanding, some patience. Whatever it is, people in the community, not just agencies and institutions, but individuals in our society must be prepared to stand behind our women in trouble. Don't listen to political hogwash telling you that mothers who find themselves without husbands are a threat to you and to all of society. Be prepared to extend at the end of your outstretched arm, not a pointing finger, but a helping hand.

Battered women do leave their abusers. Apparently in droves because that woman I mentioned in the beginning, the one who died, couldn't find room in a shelter that night. They were already full of women who had already left.

I say the question is no longer, "Why don't they leave?" I say the questions now are "Why aren't they safe when they leave?" and "What can we do to help them stay gone?"

A DEADLY CONFRONTATION

Beth Sipe

The following selection is excerpted from the book *I Am Not Your Victim: Anatomy of Domestic Violence* coauthored by Beth Sipe and Evelyn J. Hall. Sipe, who wrote the chapter from which this selection is taken, is a formerly battered woman who killed her abusive husband Steven (Sam) Sipe on April 9, 1988. Sipe recounts her experiences during the week that led up to the night she killed her husband. After sixteen years of abuse, Sipe writes, she had finally left Sam; however, the courts forced her to maintain contact with Sam so he could visit their children James and Daniel, then sixteen and eleven respectively. Sipe describes the escalation of Sam's threats, sabotage, and uncontrolled rage, as well as her increasingly desperate attempts to protect herself.

The next weekend would be Easter, and I expected a hassle from Sam about taking the boys. But, no, he surprised me by announcing he was going to Mina, Nevada, to visit his family over the weekend, and he never mentioned taking the boys along. Something about his trip plans did not ring true to me. "What is he up to now?" I wondered. When I called my attorney to report how Sam had acted Tuesday night, I also told her that some friends had invited me to bring the boys out to their country home for the Easter weekend. She encouraged me to go and to tell Sam I would be out of town. I decided to go, knowing I needed a rest from Sam's constant threats.

Death Threats

Sam's barrage of threatening calls increased during that week. Daniel visited him one day after school, as specified by the court; James refused to go. I tried to call the house on Daniel's visitation day, when I thought he should be home from school, but I could not get an answer. Finally, worried half out of my mind, I called Sam at work. He told me Daniel was supposed to go to Jane's [Sam's neighbor] to get the house key. Boy, was I furious. I thought of the way Jane treated her own kids—like dogs. She called them bastards, sons of bitches, even "little fuckers." "How can you subject Daniel to that witch?" I

From Beth Sipe, "A No-Win Result," in *I Am Not Your Victim: Anatomy of Domestic Violence*, by Beth Sipe and Evelyn J. Hall, pp. 136–44. Copyright ©1996 by Sage Publications, Inc. Reprinted by permission of Sage Publications, Inc.

asked him. Sam just laughed and hung up. Later that evening, Daniel told me that when he went to Jane and asked her for the key, she stood in her door and swore at him, told him to get over in his yard and wait for Sam.

It tore me apart to see Daniel subjected to Jane's abuse. I couldn't understand why Sam didn't give him a key to the house. I had given both boys keys to the apartment so they could get in after school whether I was there or not.

On Friday, April 1, 1988, Sam's first child-support payment was due. I felt edgy, nervous, like something bad was about to happen. Sam had been calling me and making his death threats daily, not only at home but also at work. The only way Sam could have gotten my work number was by searching through Daniel's pockets. The family I worked for saw how terrified I was. I knew that part of Sam's purpose was to upset me so much that I'd be fired. Thank God for the caring and support of these Christian people. They did not fire me. Just the opposite, they did everything they could to bolster up my spirits. While I was at work on April 1, I got a call from James reporting that Sam came to the apartment, paid $175 in cash, and made James sign a receipt for the child support. Supposedly, Sam was on his way to Mina for the weekend. I didn't know whether to feel relieved or terrified. Sam had said over and over, "I'll kill your ass before I'll pay you child support." Now he had made the first payment. It just wasn't like Sam to accept or follow the court's ruling.

Maybe I'll never know the truth about what Sam did that Easter weekend. But I'm pretty sure he didn't go to Mina. His car was parked in the drive all weekend, and I called the bus depot and learned that no bus tickets were sold to Mina. It may be difficult for someone who hasn't lived it to understand, but I felt driven to check on Sam's whereabouts because of his constant threats. Somehow I felt safer if I knew exactly where he was. My guess is that he spent the weekend with his lady friend somewhere. Anyway, the kids and I had a peaceful weekend with our friends and a special Easter dinner.

Sam's Sabotage

Monday, April 4, was my day off, and I had my usual dozen errands to do. When I tried to use my car, the whole motor began knocking. I didn't get one block from my apartment before I had to stop and push it to the curb. I asked one of my neighbors to drive it up and down the alley to listen to it, but all he could say was, "It sounds so bad I wouldn't drive it if I were you." I had it towed to the Toyota dealer where it had been repaired for the oil leaks. After checking it over, the mechanic told me, "Someone who doesn't know what they're doing has been messing with this car." Several wires had been pulled loose and one spark plug was missing. I knew I hadn't taken the car in for repairs, and the only way to open the hood was to pull a release from inside my locked car. None of the locks had been forced, so obviously, Sam had kept a duplicate key and used it to tear up my car. The bill for this repair was $225. Then I understood. He paid the $175 in child support, but made sure I had to spend it, plus some, for car repair.

The next day, James and I discovered that someone had been in the apartment. Neither of us had moved my large file of records, but it was missing. James said that all his papers and clothes had been moved around, and later I noticed that one vial of my prescription hormones had disappeared. I recall standing there as all the blood drained out of my head, feeling faint. I couldn't stop the terrible things which kept happening. Like a light bulb turning on, it hit me, "We're not safe anywhere; we'll never be safe." I called my attorney, but couldn't get past the secretary. I hoped that Connie could report Sam's stepped-up harassment to his attorney, and maybe he could stop Sam. There was nothing more I could do. I couldn't even get my phone number changed because the court ordered that Sam have the number so he could talk to the kids.

At 6 a.m. on April 6, my birthday, I answered the phone to hear Sam say, "Happy Birthday, bitch. How do you like your presents?" Then he hung up before I could say a word. I got his message alright. Sam could destroy my car, he could get into my apartment when and if he wanted, and there was nothing I could do to stop him. I felt utterly helpless, vulnerable, hopeless.

Attempts at Self-Protection

The next day, April 7, I tried again to contact Connie and again I couldn't get past her secretary. I was so exasperated I said, "Tell Connie something for me—she's fired." By this point, I had already paid Connie $500, and I certainly couldn't afford to start with another attorney. So after I fired Connie, I called Sam's lawyer myself—no need to go through a lawyer anymore since I didn't have one. I told him about my car being torn up and my apartment being rummaged. He gave me no assurances, but I sensed that he believed me when he asked if my car had been locked. He agreed that "maybe Sam was a little bit out of hand." I stressed to this lawyer to keep Sam away from me, that I had a temporary restraining order (TRO) against Sam. After talking to him, I felt a tiny ray of hope. Maybe now that Sam's attorney knew what Sam had done to me, he would take steps to stop the harassment.

My hope didn't last long. Sam was demanding that I give him my W-2 forms so that he could file a joint income tax return. I wanted to file under the option of married but separated.

Time after time, Sam called me at work during the next two days, badgering me about my W-2 forms. After hanging up from a call with him, I'd go out on the patio, trying to get control of my crying and shaking. As much as possible, I tried to protect my patients from seeing the hell I was suffering.

The next court date, April 11, was getting close, and now I had no lawyer. So I tried to gather information that I hoped would help me. I got computer printouts showing all the payments of bills for the house—the mortgage, the electric, the water softener, and so on. In the two years since we had bought the house, Sam had handled the bills. The computer printouts showed that every payment on every bill had been late. I inquired of John Hancock Insurance Company whether or not Sam had kept the policies on me and the boys in force since we had moved out of the house. Their representative informed me that our policies were still in force. In fact, Sam had increased the death benefits of my policy from $10,000 to $100,000. This was one more indication to me that Sam's threats to kill me were serious.

Hopelessness and Desperation

It was Sam's weekend to have Daniel, so Daniel went directly from school to Sam's on Friday, April 8. But Sam called me several times during that day and night. His threats were so menacing that I called the Domestic Crisis Hotline. There wasn't much they could do for me except listen, because my boys were too old to be admitted to the shelter, and I wasn't willing to leave without the boys.

Again on Saturday, April 9, Sam called me at work, threatening me so forcefully that I finally gave in and told him, "OK, you can take the W-2s if you'll promise to leave me alone." I don't know how I got through work that day as upset as I was.

I arrived home about 5:30 p.m. As I had every day for at least three months, I carried my gun with me, reassembling and loading it when I got into the apartment. I sat down on my bed, which was in the living room, and stuck the gun under it. I tried to call my sister in Arkansas as I did every other weekend, but her line was busy. I went into the kitchen to start cooking supper, taking the gun with me. The gun had become a part of me, like my arms and legs. James came home from seeing one of his friends, and we talked briefly, just catching up on the day. Then Daniel called to ask if he could be a few minutes late. "Sure," I told him, "today's Saturday, no school tomorrow." Sam got on the phone, talking sticky sweet, asking would I get the W-2s ready and would James be there. I asked James while Sam was still on the phone and James said no. Sam's voice took on a sharp edge as he pressured me to make James stay. I told Sam that was James's decision.

The Final Confrontation

Sam must have called from a phone booth near by, because within ten or fifteen minutes they were there. James started out the door as Sam and Daniel were coming in. Sam grabbed him by the shoulder and asked him to stay, but James pulled away from him. Daniel was showing James a squirt gun Sam had given him. That was a slap in the face to me; Sam knew I didn't allow the boys to have toy guns. After a brief exchange with Daniel, James went on his way.

I was watching Sam intently. I had asked him not to come in, to stand outside the door while I got the W-2s for him. Sam continued into the apartment as Daniel hugged me around the waist, telling me about playing racquetball. Sam's voice turned gruff as he said, "Go to your room, Daniel." I knew then that he meant to hurt me. "I got you now, bitch," he said. "You don't have a lawyer and you can't afford to hire another one." I started crying as I asked him, "Why are you doing this to me, to your kids? How can you love them and do this? My God, your own son just walked by you, didn't even want to see you. If I just leave, not take the kids or anything, then will you leave me alone?" He was standing there real stiff, gritting his teeth, fists flailing, his eyes glaring with hate. "Never," he said, "never." He was between me and the door, and all I could think about was getting him out of my apartment. "Just take the W-2s and get out," I told him, hoping that would break up the argument. I backed away from him to the end of my bed and bent over to get the forms from my briefcase. I only took my eyes off him for a moment as I opened the briefcase.

Suddenly, he grabbed me by my hair and one shoulder and slammed my head down full force on the end table. Again, my head hit the table, another explosion in my head. I was foggy, almost blacked out, for a moment. My stomach came up in my throat as if I were on a roller coaster. I became aware of wetness; I had wet my pants. "Dear God, he really is going to kill me and he wanted both boys here. Why? So they would see it, or did he mean to kill them too?" So many thoughts flooding my mind at once.

Sam had me from the back, so I couldn't fight or protect myself. I felt a surge of adrenaline. I was never so strong in my life as I pulled away from him enough to grab a flowerpot and hit him with it. I'm not sure where it hit him, but I know I tried for his head. He let go then. I staggered back by the bed, reached down, and got my gun. Sam was facing me, arms out like a football tackle, coming at me. I pointed the gun at him and told him to just get out. He smirked as he kept coming. Scenes from the past flashed through my mind, times when Sam had simply reached out and taken the gun away from me. As I backed up, I said, "Please don't make me do this; please don't make me." I backed up more until I felt the bed touching my legs. I looked over at the phone, a long way away. I felt my body begin to pitch backward. I had one arm out to keep from falling because I knew he'd be right on me.

Sam kept coming, saying, "Get you, bitch! Get you, bitch!"

All I remember is screaming, screaming, screaming, and the sound of gunshots as if from far away. I can still see him coming toward me. Another shot, and he sort of reeled like maybe he was hit, but he was still coming toward me. More gunshots, I must have fired them, then I didn't see him anymore. I remember thinking just pull the gun up to your head and fire one time, just one time. I tried, but the gun clicked empty.

Then I heard Daniel screaming. I didn't know at that moment where I was. I remember blinking my eyes, trying to focus. I saw Daniel, standing near where Sam had been. I didn't even know he was in the room. He was screaming, "Mom, Mom!" The room was like a tunnel filled with gray, fuzzy fog. All I could see was Daniel going out the door, and I ran after him. Daniel was running down the alley screaming, and I was running behind him, yelling, "Stop, Daniel, stop." When I realized I still had the gun in my hand, I flung it away from me and continued running after Daniel. I knew I had to catch him and calm him before he reached Washington Street with its heavy traffic. Just as we got to Washington, I caught him. We were both screaming for help. I was short of breath, and my head felt like it was filled with cotton. We started back holding each other. As we approached the apartments, Daniel broke away and ran back into our apartment, while a young couple helped me upstairs to their apartment. I kept asking them to help me get back to my apartment because I was worried about Daniel being in there alone with Sam. I tried to walk but my legs buckled under me and I fainted.

When I came to, I was on the floor. Two policemen came in then and took me out on the patio to question me. I was shaking all over, my fingers and toes tingling from lack of circulation, my mouth so dry I had to pull my lips away from my teeth to talk. Someone gave me a glass of water. I told them I had fired the gun and wasn't sure whether or not I had hit Sam. My head was throbbing and I felt sick all over. One officer said to the other, "Maybe we'd better get her to a hospital," but the other said, "That can wait." I heard a lot of sirens and a helicopter hovering overhead. There were lights everywhere. I asked how Sam was, but the officers didn't answer me. When they told me they were taking me to the police station, I asked if I could change my clothes and grab my purse. They refused, so I had to go in my wet pants without my purse. They wouldn't even let me see or be with Daniel. My baby, my poor baby, what was happening to him? This all seemed so foggy, so unreal. Was I dreaming or was I crazy?

At the police station, they put me in an outer office and gave me some coffee. I told them I was hurt. My eyes wouldn't stay focused. After a while—I have no idea how long—they allowed me to go to the bathroom. I was bent over with the dry heaves, and when I straightened up, I saw myself in the mirror. I could barely tell it was me. My hair was pulled loose and stringy; my left temple bore a large raw bloody sore; red and blue splotches covered my entire face, with a larger one on my forehead; large swollen knots oozing blood covered my head.

The same two officers who had brought me in began questioning

me. Repeatedly they told me to speak up, but my throat was so sore
from screaming I could barely speak above a whisper. I asked them
over and over about Sam. Once they told me he was in surgery, but
mostly, they said, "No word." I prayed with all my strength, "Please,
God, let Sam be alive; don't let me have killed someone. God, send
me to prison for life; just don't let Sam die."

After what seemed an eternity, one of the officers told me Sam was
dead. I remember looking at my right hand and thinking, "Cut it off,
look what it did. I've killed someone, not just anyone, but Sam. I still
have all this love for him, and now he's made me kill him." Feelings
of horror and grief overwhelmed me.

One detective told me it looked like self-defense, but that I had to
make a statement or they would be forced to lock me up until I could
get a lawyer. I asked permission to call a lawyer but was told I couldn't
until I was formally booked into jail. While this was soaking in, they
went on to say they didn't know what would happen to Daniel. He
was upset enough without knowing his father was dead. And if I
didn't cooperate, Daniel would be sent to Child Haven. They told me
they had James's personal phone book and had been calling around
trying to find him with no success. "He's liable to hear this on the
news," they told me, "Is that what you want? We'll have to call Juvenile Center and put both boys in there if you don't cooperate. The
sooner you accept that and give us a statement, the sooner you'll be
out of here to take care of your sons." I could hear Daniel crying off
and on from another room. But the officers wouldn't let me see him if
I didn't talk. It felt like blackmail.

My brain was on overload—hundreds of thoughts about Sam,
Daniel, James tumbling around in my mind. The uniformed officer
was in the questioning room with me, his head down, arms crossed,
shaking his head, while the two detectives stood against the wall. I
had the distinct impression that he didn't approve of the detectives'
coercive methods. But I answered all their questions truthfully and
signed a release for medical records. Even when I finished all that,
they wouldn't let me see Daniel for another hour.

Finally, they let me in the room where they were holding Daniel.
He cried as he hugged me and said, "Mom, it's not your fault; he was
beating on you—he wouldn't stop." Daniel didn't know that Sam was
dead, and I didn't want to tell him at the police station while he was
so upset. I sat there holding Daniel, trying to comfort him, until one
of the detectives took us home.

It was around 2 a.m. when we got back to the apartment; Sam had
arrived there about 8 p.m.

I couldn't grasp what had happened. Sam was dead and I had killed
him. In the span of one evening, our lives were turned upside down.
And the future loomed ahead as an endless black hole, just as terrifying as Sam's sixteen-year reign of terror.

FROM BATTERED WOMAN TO ADVOCATE

Hara Estroff Marano

Hara Estroff Marano is the editor of the popular psychology magazine *Psychology Today*. In the following selection, she reviews the life of public prosecutor Sarah Buel, an advocate for battered women who was also once abused. Marano writes that Buel remembers what it was like to be afraid, with no one to help, and no options but to go back to her abuser; however, Buel managed to escape her abuser and eventually graduated from Harvard Law School. According to Marano, these experiences fueled Buel's broad approach toward the advocacy of battered women. For example, Marano writes, Buel not only helps her own clients escape abuse, but she also tries to reach other battered women by educating legal and medical professionals about recognizing and dealing with abuse.

Whatever else American culture envisions of petite blondes, it doesn't expect them to end up as social revolutionaries. But just that turn of fate has brought Sarah Buel to Williamsburg, Virginia, from suburban Boston, where she is assistant district attorney of Norfolk County. To a gathering of judges, lawyers, probation and police officers, victim advocates, and others, she has come to press an idea that meets persistent resistance—to explain why and, perhaps more importantly, precisely how domestic violence should be handled, namely as the serious crime that it is, an assault with devastating effects against individuals, families, and communities, now and for generations to come.

Buel, 41, a speed talker—there is, after all, so much to say—tells them what Los Angeles prosecutors failed to explain in the O.J. Simpson case [Simpson was acquitted in October 1995 of the murder of his ex-wife, Nicole Brown Simpson, and her friend, Ronald Goldman]: how batterers cannily dodge responsibility for their own actions, as if other people sneak into their brains and ball their fingers into fists, how they are deft at shifting the blame to others, especially their mates; how they watch and stalk partners, even those under the protection of the court, and especially those who have separated or divorced. Instead of holding up Simpson as the poster boy for domestic violence, the California trial let him get away with doing what batterers almost always do—put on a great public face and portray themselves as victims.

The judges and cops and court officers pay attention to Buel because domestic violence is a daily hassle that takes a lot out of them. And if there's one thing Buel knows, it's how batterers manipulate the law enforcement system. They listen because Buel has that most unassailable credential, an honors degree from Harvard Law School. But mostly they listen because Buel has been on the receiving end of a fist.

"Sometimes I hate talking about it," she confides. "I just want people to see me as the best trial lawyer." But, as Deborah D. Tucker says, "she grabs them by the heart." Tucker, head of the Texas Council on Family Violence and chairman of the national committee that pushed the Violence Against Women Act into the 1994 Omnibus Crime Bill, explains: "She gets people to feel what they need to feel to be vulnerable to the message that domestic violence is not we/they. Any of us can become victimized. It's not about the woman. It's about the culture."

Speaking Up

Certainly Buel never had any intention of speaking publicly about her own abuse. It started accidentally. She was in a court hallway with some police officers on a domestic violence case. "See, a smart woman like you would never let this happen," the chief said, gesturing her way. And in an instant Buel made a decision that changed her life irrevocably, and the lives of many others. "Well, it did happen," she told him, challenging his blame-the-victim tone. He invited her to train his force on handling domestic violence. "It changed things completely. I decided I had an obligation to speak up. It's a powerful tool."

It has made her a star, says psychologist David Adams, Ed.D. By speaking from her own experience, Buel reminds people that law can be a synonym for justice. In conferences and in courts, she has gotten even the most cynical judges to listen to battered women—instead of blaming them. "I am amazed at how often people are sympathetic as long as the victim closely resembles Betty Crocker. I worry about the woman who comes into court who doesn't look so pretty. Maybe she has a tattoo or dreadlocks. I want judges to stop wondering, 'What did she do to provoke him?'" Sarah Buel is arguably the country's sharpest weapon against domestic violence.

Buel finishes her talk, and in the split second before the audience jumps to its feet cheering, you can hear people gasp "Whew!" Not because they're tired of sitting, but because in her soft but hurried tones, the prosecution of batterers takes on a passionate, even optimistic, urgency. It's possible, she feels, to end domestic violence, although not by prosecution alone. Buel does not dwell on herself as victim but transmutes her own experience into an aria of hope, a recipe for change, "so that any woman living in despair knows there's help."

Not like she knew. She herself was clueless.

One of five children, Buel was born in Chicago but moved endlessly with her family from the age of four. Her father, an auto mechanic fond of drink, always felt success lay elsewhere. Her mother, a Holocaust refugee who fled Austria as a child, went along selflessly—"she didn't know how to speak up," says Buel, which fueled her own desire to do so.

In the seventh grade, Buel was put on a secretarial track. "I was told I wasn't smart enough. So I refused to learn how to type." When she was 14, her parents divorced. Rather than choose which one to live with (her siblings split evenly), Buel headed for New York.

She went to school—at first—while working as a governess. For the first time, she saw television and while watching Perry Mason decided "this is what I want to do." The next year Buel bounced around to four different schools and families, including her mother's. "I went home for three months, but it was too different," she recalls.

Becoming a Battered Woman

Buel eventually went back to New York, where she had relatives, and began a very erratic course through high school, cutting class and shoplifting with a cousin. By the time she was 22, Buel was an abused woman. It came completely out of the blue. She was listening to a song on the radio, "Jeremiah Was a Bullfrog." "I bet that makes you think of Jeremy [a boyfriend of hers way back when she was 15]," her partner said. Actually what she was thinking was how stupid the song was. "Admit it," he insisted, "it does, doesn't it?" No, she said, it doesn't. He accused her of lying—and slapped her across the face.

The verbal and psychological abuse proved more damaging than the physical abuse. There was endless criticism. "He always said I looked frumpy and dumpy. He was enraged if I bought the *New York Times*." He read the tabloid *Daily News*. "'Isn't it good enough for you?' he demanded. He was extremely jealous. If I so much as commented on, say a man's coat, he'd accuse me of wanting an affair and flirting. If I wanted to take courses, he insisted the only reason was to flirt with other men. I didn't cook like his mother, clean like his mother. By the time I left I thought, 'The only thing I do well is, I'm a good mother.'"

Suddenly Buel is surprised to find herself revealing this much personal detail. "I never tell other women the details of my own abuse. They'll measure. Was theirs more or less?"

In 1993 and 1994, a coveted Bunting fellowship from Radcliffe College allowed Buel to work only part time as a public prosecutor. Now, in between court appearances, she crisscrosses the country, finally able to accept invitations to train judges and address gatherings such as this, a first-ever assembly of Virginians Against Domestic Violence. She has visited 49 states. She has testified before Congress. She was even asked to introduce the president of the United States at a press conference in the spring of 1995, when the federal government set up a new Violence Against Women Office.

But no matter who she talks to or what she says about domestic violence, "it always comes down to one thing," says Buel. "They all ask the same question: Why do they [the women] stay."

First she points out that there are half as many shelters for battered women as there are for stray animals—about 1,800—and most do not accept children. For every two women sheltered, five are turned away. For every two children sheltered, eight are turned away.

A Texas study shows that 75 percent of victims calling domestic violence hotlines had left at least five times. Buel herself first went to the Legal Aid Society. There was a three-year wait for help. They never informed her about safety, never told her about alternatives. She did see a counselor at a family center, but her partner wouldn't go; he would only drive her.

Why Leaving Was Difficult

Buel left her abuser and got a job in a shoe factory. But the wage was so low she couldn't pay the rent and a baby-sitter. "I went back because he said he was sorry, it'll never happen again. When I realized it wasn't true, I left again. I told him I was packing to go to my brother's wedding. I took a bus to New Hampshire, where my mother lived. That didn't work out—she was living on a remote farm, I had no car, and my son was allergic to many of the animals—but I never went back. So 18 years ago I stood on a welfare line with three kids, my own son and two foster children I was raising. But you can't live on that amount of money. We trade our safety for poverty. We go back because we don't know what else to do."

Batterers are expert at portraying themselves as the injured party. The first time her batterer threw her against a wall, Buel's son screamed, "Don't hurt my mom." Then the batterer shouted, "See, you're turning the kid against me."

"I used to think, 'Why me? I must have done something terrible.' Women come to think it was their fault. They feel guilty for not doing a good enough job as a mom because they are unable to protect themselves, or their children."

A major obstacle to leaving, says Buel, is battered women's fear of losing their children or of being unable to protect them. "A Massachusetts study documented that in 70 percent of cases where fathers attempted to get custody of their children, they did so successfully. So when the abuser says to her, 'Sure, you can leave, but I've got the money to hire a good lawyer and I'll get the kids,' he may be right.

"We go back because we think we'll figure out a way to stop the violence, the magic secret everybody else seems to know. We don't want to believe that our marriage or relationship failed because we weren't willing to try just a little harder. I felt deeply ashamed, that it must be my fault. I never heard anyone else talking about it. I assumed I was the only one it was happening to."

One of the biggest reasons women stay, says Buel, is that they are most vulnerable when they leave. That's when abusers desperately escalate tactics of control. More domestic abuse victims are killed when fleeing than at any other time.

A Memory of Terror

Buel has a crystal-clear memory of a Saturday morning at the laundromat with her young son, in the small New Hampshire town where she had fled, safely, she thought, far from her abuser. "I saw my ex-partner, coming in the door. There were people over by the counter and I yelled to them to call the police, but my ex-partner said, 'No, this is my woman. We've just had a little fight and I've come to pick her up. Nobody needs to get involved.' I still had bruises on the side of my face, and I said, 'No, this is the person who did this to me, you need to call the police.' But he said, 'No, this is my woman. Nobody needs to get involved.' Nobody moved. And I thought, as long as I live I want to remember what it feels like to be terrified for my life while nobody even bothers to pick up the phone."

It's time, Buel sighs, to stop asking why they stay and start asking what they need to feel safe. "I'm obsessed with safety now," she confides. "More important than prosecution, more important than anything, is a safety plan, an action plan detailing how to stay alive." And so a first encounter with a victim requires a verbal walk-through of what she'll need to feel safe at her place of work, at home, on the streets, and suggestions about what she'll need for leaving—birth certificates, legal papers, bank accounts—and for dealing with the abuser.

Buel entered Harvard Law in 1987. "I would love to have gone sooner but I had no idea how to get there. I didn't know you had to go to college to go to law school." She imagined you first had to work long enough as a legal secretary. In 1977, after two months on welfare, Buel entered a federally funded job-training program that, despite her awful typing, landed her in a legal services office. Eventually, she became a paralegal aide and began helping domestic violence victims.

In 1980, she started seven years of undergraduate study, first at Columbia University on scholarship, which necessitated "nine horrible months" in a drug-ridden building in New York while on welfare, so that instead of working nights she could spend them with her son. Ultimately she returned to New England and, two nights a week, attended Harvard Extension School, a vastly different world from Harvard Yard. She did well.

Days were spent working as a women's advocate in federal legal services offices, first in New Hampshire, then in grimy Lowell, Massachusetts. Buel started shelters and hotlines for battered women. She helped draft an abuse prevention law. She dreamed about being a voice for the women she represented.

Fulfilling a Dream

She learned to write. She took classes in public speaking. Toward the end of her undergraduate studies, her bosses asked her where she wanted to go to law school. "Harvard," she replied, "because they're rich and they'll give me money." The lawyers laughed and told her that wasn't how it worked: "They do the choosing, not you." They took pains to point out she just wasn't Harvard material. "You're a single mother. You've been on welfare. You're too old."

Angry and humiliated, Buel began a private campaign that typifies her fierce determination. In the dark after classes, she drove around the law school, shouting at it: "You're going to let me in." Soon she got braver and stopped the car to go inside and look around. Then she had to see what it was like to sit in a classroom. She decided if she ever got accepted, she'd choose one of the orange-colored lockers, because her son was a fan of the Syracuse Orangemen.

Harvard Law not only accepted Buel but gave her a full scholarship. Once there, she was surprised there was nothing in the criminal-law syllabus about family violence—this despite the fact that women are more likely to be the victim of a crime in their own home, at the hands of someone they know, than on the streets. Buel mentioned the oversight to her professor. He told her to take over the class for one hour one day. She thought she'd be educating movers and shakers for the future. "I was amazed when, during the next six weeks, no less than 16 classmates came up to me either because they were in violent relationships or their parents or friends were."

When Boston-area colleagues requested help on an advocacy program for battered women and she couldn't do it alone, Buel put an ad in the student newspaper; 78 volunteers showed up for the first meeting. By year's end there were 215. She started a pro bono legal counseling program. The Battered Women's Advocacy Project is now the largest student program at Harvard Law; a quarter of the participants are men.

In 1990, at age 36, Buel graduated, cum laude. She sent a copy of her transcript to her old junior-high teacher with a note suggesting that she not judge the future of 12-year-old girls.

Giving Women Options

At first Buel thought it would be enough to become a prosecutor and make sure that batterers are held accountable for assaulting others. But she has come to see it differently. "That's not enough. My role is not just to make women safe but to see that they are financially empowered and that they have a life plan." So every morning, from 8:30 to 9:15, before court convenes, she sees that all women there on domestic issues are briefed, given a complete list of resources, training options, and more. "We surveyed battered women. We asked them what they needed to know. I wanted everyone to listen to them. Usually no one ever does. Most people tell them what to do. 'Leave him.' 'Do this.' 'Do that.' You can't tell women to leave until you give them—with their children—a place to go, the knowledge how and the resources to get by on their own, and the safety to do so. It's all about options."

What's more, Buel now sees domestic violence as just one arc of a much bigger cycle, intimately connected to all violence, and that it takes a whole coordinated community effort to stop it, requiring the participation of much more than attorneys and judges. It takes everyone; even the locksmith, so that when a woman suddenly needs her locks changed, the call will be heeded.

Rather than drive her own career narrowly forward, Buel has instead broadened her approach, venturing into places few lawyers ever go. She regularly attends community council meetings in Germantown, a dreary outpost of public housing in Quincy, Massachusetts, known for its high crime rate. The council—Head Start teachers, the parish priest, two cops who requested duty in the projects, a few community members—celebrates mundane triumphs. A parents dinner at Head Start. A potluck supper at the church.

Buel is absolutely certain that this is the real answer to crime. It is the prevailing fallacy to assume that big problems require big solutions. First a community has to knit itself together—and from the sound of things the best way is on its stomach. "People here hear that some things are unacceptable," says one. A cop reports, remarkably, there has not been a single incident in a month.

Buel tells the assembled that emergency housing funds are available for battered women whose husbands are not paying support. "This is how I get the dirt on what's going on," she tells me. "These officers will call me when there's a domestic violence problem but the woman isn't ready to enter the legal system. At least we can keep an eye on her, and the children, to make sure she's safe."

Buel is particularly concerned about the children. She knows that children who witness violence become violent themselves. "Some take on the role of killing their mother's batterer," says Buel, who notes that 63 percent of males between ages 11 and 20 who are doing time for homicide have killed their mother's batterer. "We adults have abdicated the role of making the home safe.". . .

An Unconventional Lawyer

For her unusually diversified approach to domestic violence, Buel gives full credit to William Delahunt, her boss, the district attorney. "He has allowed me to challenge the conventional notion of what our job is."

"My boss gets complaints about me all the time," Buel says proudly. There was the batterer who, despite divorce and remarriage, was thought to be the source of menacing gifts anonymously sent to his ex-wife—a gun box for Christmas, a bullet box for Valentine's Day, followed by the deeds to burial plots for her and her new husband. The woman repeatedly hauled her ex into court for violating a restraining order; one lawyer after another got him off. "Finally I got him for harassing her in the parking garage where she was going to college; of course he denied it. The lawyer contended she was making up all the stories. But a detective found a videotape from the garage, which corroborated her charge. In the appeals court, his lawyer, a big guy, leaned into my face and hissed, 'You may be a good little advocate for your cause, but you're a terrible lawyer.'" She won the appeal.

Because the students asked for one, Buel teaches a class on domestic violence to 43 students at Boston College Law School. Over a third of them are males.

And she lectures widely to the medical profession. "Doctors see abused women all the time and don't know it," she says. She is especially interested in reaching family doctors and obstetrician/gynecologists, because in over a third of instances, abuse occurs during pregnancy—as it did for her. It is the primary time for the onset of violence. Her goal is to see that all doctors routinely ask every woman at every visit whether she has been hit or threatened since her last visit, explain that they are now routinely asking the question, state that no woman deserves to be abused, and then provide information and referral if she has. This simple question, by exposing abuse to plain daylight, brilliantly erases some of its shame. It is only when shame is gone that abused women can ask for help. . . .

Focusing on What Works

In her travels, Buel has observed firsthand that many jurisdictions have figured out how to reduce violence against women. She sees her mission as spreading the word about them. Buel's considerable charisma stems in no small measure from her conviction that the solutions are out there, if only everyone knew about them. "People are always surprised at my optimism," she says.

"There's no one solution," she insists. "You need a message from the whole community. People point to the policy of mandatory arrest of all batterers in Duluth, Minnesota. But Duluth also has billboards that warn, 'Never hit a child.'" Buel's list of what works includes:

- the end of silence about spouse abuse.
- probation officers sensitive to the safety needs of victims and serious monitoring of offenders.
- mandatory group treatment programs for batterers. Programs must last at least a year, hold them alone accountable, and teach

them to respect women.
- sanctions for failure to comply with probation or restraining orders.
- the use of advocates to follow cases.
- training cops in how to investigate and gather complete evidence when answering domestic violence calls.

Buel waves an investigation checklist she got from police in San Diego. If information gathering is done correctly, prosecution can proceed even when the victim refuses to press charges or come to court as a witness. "When a woman refuses to testify, she's not 'failing to cooperate,'" she says. "She's terrified. She's making the statement, 'I want to stay alive.'"

I ask Buel about her working relationships with judges. "In Massachusetts, I'm characterized as too harsh. I simply ask for some mechanism of accountability. Judges here are appointed for life without mandatory training. Many come from the big law firms that represent the batterers. Some do a great job. Others lose sight of the victims and children."

Discrimination against women through the law infuriates Buel. A recent study shows that a batterer who kills his wife typically gets a jail term of two to four years. But a woman who kills her abuser gets 14 to 18 years.

Of course, a great deal of domestic violence never finds its way into the criminal justice system; it's handled by private psychotherapists. "No one wants her husband arrested," especially women from the upper income strata, says Buel. She regrets that she is rarely invited to speak to the mental health community.

"Unfortunately," she charges, "most therapists, including family counselors, have little training in domestic violence. They are often conned by the stories of the batterers, experts at shifting blame. Without realizing it, therapists often put women at greater risk of abuse. There is nothing victims can disclose to them for which there will not be later retaliation. At the very least, therapists don't think in terms of safety plans for the victims.

"Batterers are extraordinarily talented in sucking in therapists, the community, even their wives' families. Their whole M.O. is manipulation. They'll get the priest to testify that they're family-loving men, but the priest isn't there during the abuse. They are notorious liars; they'll say whatever makes them look good. Even if the woman gets a restraining order barring her partner from having any contact with her, these guys will make calls or send flowers. They're not really showing love, just proving they can get around the system, showing who's boss." In the toxic world of domestic violence, simply receiving an unsigned birthday card can be a deadly threat.

Yet domestic violence thrives in the best of zip codes, including the bedroom communities for Boston's medical chiefs. "Two of the worst cases I ever prosecuted involved doctors," says Buel, who finds that domestic violence is increasing in severity among wealthier families. "There's a much greater use of weapons. Ten years ago you would never have heard of a computer executive putting a gun to his wife's head."

Because too many victims stay with their batterers, Buel has begun to radically shift her approach to ending violence. "I'm learning new ways to compromise, reaching out to defense attorneys." In this she is crossing a divide most feminist lawyers shun. The defense attorneys, after all, represent batterers, "because they have the money." But they also have some power over their clients. "Some defense attorneys are willing to change their practices, to agree to take on batterers only if they go to a treatment program and stick with it."

This braving of the breach gives the lie to any suggestion that Buel is motivated by vindictiveness. She rolls her huge eyes at characterizations of activists as man haters. Or as do-gooders blind to the "fact" that people don't change. . . .

The Life of an Advocate

Returning to Boston from Williamsburg, Buel attends back-to-back meetings. First is the board session of a foundation that funds battered-women's shelters. Next comes the Domestic Violence Council, a regional group of private and public attorneys who share information and strategies. Buel started the council in law school. It has grown exponentially since, and now meets at one of Boston's prestige law firms. Discussions this day focus on:

- Lawyers' safety. Being the barrier between a woman and her batterer sometimes leads to threats, or worse; victims and their attorneys have been murdered—even in the courthouse. A lawyer reports that her tires were punctured.
- A new cultural trend toward what look like organizations for the preservation of fatherhood. Masquerading as involved fathers, members are often batterers who use their kids as a way of stalking or threatening ex-partners. A law student assigned to check out one group's roster reports that 86 percent of the men have restraining orders against them.
- Monitoring the courts. For two years, practicing and student attorneys have been trained to evaluate how the state's judges handle domestic violence cases. Now they're assembling a committee to meet with those doing a bad job—those who, say, don't ask about kids or weapons when considering requests for restraining orders—and inform them how to do better.

The day has no end. Dinner isn't simply a meal, it's an opportunity to give support and advice to two Harvard Law grads who have formed the fledgling Women's Rights Network. Where should they go for funding? Does she know a defense attorney in Edmonton (Canada) for the international information they are putting together on domestic violence?

And Buel whips out some formidable pieces of paper, legal-pad sheets neatly filled with the names and phone numbers of people—73 per side—whose calls she must return. There were, I think, four of them, neatly written, neatly folded, representing two or three days' worth of calls to her office and her home. She keeps her number listed so women in trouble can find her. Somewhere on the list is an Edmonton attorney.

THE LUCKIEST DAY OF HIS LIFE

Bill Ibelle

In the following selection, Bill Ibelle interviews a former batterer, Donald, and his wife. Donald describes the five years during which he abused his wife, his arrest, his experiences in the treatment program, and the changes he has made in his relationship with his wife. Donald's wife also tells Ibelle her perspective of what it was like to be a victim of abuse. Donald explains that he learned in treatment that batterers must learn to take full responsibility for the beatings rather than finding someone else to blame. Despite the poor prognosis for most batterers, Donald believes that his arrest and his subsequent participation in a batterer treatment program has resulted in a lasting change in his behavior. Ibelle is a staff writer for the *Standard-Times*, the daily newspaper of New Bedford and other south coast communities in Massachusetts.

Donald beat his wife.

He gave her black eyes, silenced her with looks of impending rage, insisted on controlling her every move, and ensured all this remained a secret by isolating her from friends and family.

He was, in short, a batterer: one of a group of men who cause more injuries to women in this country than car accidents, muggings and rapes combined, according to statistics compiled by the National Women's Health Resource Center.

The prognosis for batterers is not good. Even the best estimates put the success rate at around 40 percent, and success is defined as refraining from violence for just one year.

But unlike most batterers, Donald changed his ways in 1994 after he was arrested, sent to jail and ordered to enroll in a batterers' treatment program at the Community Center for Non-Violence in New Bedford, Massachusetts.

Today Donald and his wife agree that the violence has stopped, their relationship has improved and their two small daughters are growing up in a much healthier environment.

Donald—who agreed to be interviewed under the condition that

Reprinted, with permission, from Bill Ibelle, "Donald Says the Day of His Arrest Was the Luckiest Day of His Life," *New Bedford (Mass.) Standard Times*, May 26, 1995.

his last name not be used—credits the police, the courts and the treatment program for this dramatic turn of events.

"I'm glad the law finally stopped me," he said. "They locked me up for six months and it changed my life. If I hadn't stopped when I did, it only would have gotten worse. Sooner or later she would have gotten really hurt. I really believe that."

Five Years of Abuse

Donald said he abused his wife throughout their five-year marriage.

It could start with anything—a minor offhand comment from his wife, a late dinner; sometimes he would be angry because they didn't have money to pay the rent.

"When he got like that, I knew there was a beating coming on," said his wife, who asked that her name not be used. "At times I'd be so scared I'd be shaking inside. Sometimes I'd think, maybe I should just kill myself before he gets home—just to get it over with."

According to Donald, the beatings, the verbal abuse and the intimidation were all about control.

"It was like having a new toy," he said. "I had the buttons and I could make her do whatever I wanted. I was trying to intimidate her. I wanted to control her for the simple reason that I knew I could do it. It made me feel powerful."

Whenever Donald's wife left the house, he gave her a specific amount of time to complete the excursion. If she was late, he beat her. But most of the time he didn't have to, because the mere threat of abuse was enough to make his wife toe the line.

"I'd be at my girlfriend's looking at my watch the whole time because I knew that if I was late, I'd get hit," she said.

The longer the abuse continued, the tighter the controls became.

"Pretty soon, I didn't have any friends," she said. "I'd be invited to parties but I always made up an excuse. I never brought anyone to my house. He even stopped me from talking to anyone in the family because he was scared I'd tell someone."

While the actual physical abuse was sporadic, the psychological abuse was relentless. Whenever Donald drank, his rage bubbled dangerously close to the surface. This alone was enough to make his wife cower in his presence.

"He'd growl like a monster," she said. "I was too terrified to get help because I figured I'd get killed when I got back. So I never told anyone he hit me."

Like many batterers, Donald was highly manipulative and had a keen sense of when he had pushed his wife too far. Whenever she was about to leave, he would apologize, shower her with presents and tell her how much he loved her and the kids.

"I'd con my way right out of it," he said. "I conned everyone. At work I was just a fun-loving guy. No one would have ever suspected the way I was at home. It felt good. But it finally caught up with me."

The first two times Donald was arrested, his wife refused to cooperate with the police so he was charged with disorderly conduct, taken into protective custody and released the next day.

Meanwhile, the abuse escalated. Not only was Donald's wife in mortal danger, so was Donald.

"I thought 'I'll just kill him. That will solve everything. I'll kill him and then go right to the police and tell them what I'd done and why I did it,'" she said.

The Arrest

Luckily for both of them, the law stepped in before it was too late. While Donald's wife was out getting a pizza for the family, she ran into some police officers she knew from working the night shift at a local doughnut shop. The officers saw the bruises on her face and convinced her to give a statement about the abuse at home. The bruises and her story were all the police needed to take action.

When Donald's wife arrived home with the pizza, the police were already leading him out of the house in handcuffs and the kids were asking where the men were taking daddy.

Donald was sentenced to 1½ years in jail. He was released after six months in an intensive alcohol program under the condition that he enroll immediately in batterers treatment.

Unlike many others, Donald entered the Community Center for Non-Violence determined to turn his life around. He was horrified that his daughter watched the police haul him off to jail in handcuffs and that he missed his other daughter's first birthday. In spite of the years of abuse, his wife stuck by him even after his arrest. That, too, filled him with remorse.

"She had every right to leave," he said. "I put her through hell. I assumed it was over but she came to visit me every week. That made me feel bad. I owe her for that. I swore that will never happen again."

During the first portion of the batterers program, group members are confronted with their deeds. The goal is to make them accept responsibility for their actions—to stop blaming their partners, booze, their temper.

"They continually stressed that it was our behavior that got us into this situation," said Donald. "It's not what she did or what she said—we had to take responsibility for our actions."

Taking full responsibility for the beatings is a key hurdle to graduating to the second part of the treatment program. Because he had already admitted his problem, this took Donald only four weeks.

But most men arrive at batterers treatment convinced that someone else is to blame—their partner, the police, the judge. For these men, it can take several months to get past the first stage of treatment. Some never make it and wind up back in jail.

During the second portion of the treatment program, men focus more on finding the source of their violence and ways to manage their rage. They discuss attitudes toward women and their demand for total control. They explore their childhood, the way their parents treated each other and the attitudes and communication patterns they learned in childhood.

"When I first got into the program I didn't know what to expect," said Donald. "I couldn't imagine sharing my problems with a bunch of strangers. But this is something I needed for myself and my kids. I was there to get the help. I wasn't going to let this happen to my kids again."

As the men explore these issues, they also learn relaxation techniques, ways to recognize the warning signs of building rage and ways to diffuse that rage. They learn better ways of communicating with their partner to avoid unnecessary battles and develop a richer relationship.

Learning the Victim's Perspective

Half way through the program, clients at the local women's center discuss domestic violence from the victim's perspective.

"It was terrifying—especially hearing about the children," said Donald. "She told us stories that made my skin crawl. They made me take a good look at myself. It put a real bad guilt on me."

Donald has a tough time putting into words what he got out of the program. He says he learned that his wife is a human being too. That may not sound like much, but experts say that this is a huge step for many batterers.

"I learned that it takes two people to make a relationship," he said. "I didn't let her do anything. I said it was all a man's job. Now I realize I have a partner in this marriage and I better learn to talk."

Donald's wife agrees their relationship has improved. She is included in the decision making and has more personal freedom. Since Donald completed the program, she has enrolled at Fisher College to become a medical assistant.

"I never would have allowed that before," said Donald. "I was the working man and I wanted her home getting supper on the table."

He has stopped drinking and learned to control his temper. When he feels himself losing control, he leaves the situation and comes back later to discuss the disagreement. When he talks with his wife, he actually listens to her.

As a result, the entire family's life has improved dramatically.

In the first five years of their marriage, they lived in six different apartments because Donald kept losing jobs and falling behind in the rent.

Since he completed the alcohol program, Donald has found a lucrative welding job, bought a house and a new car.

"Since all this happened I've changed a lot," he said. "I don't think I'll ever relapse. I know I'd lose everything—this house, these kids, her—everything. I still have a lot to prove to a lot of people. But the most important people I've got to prove it to are me and her. I'm not going to blow it this time."

He paused.

"I just hope it stops here. I don't want my daughters to grow up and get married and end up going through this same thing."

ORGANIZATIONS TO CONTACT

The editors have compiled the following list of organizations concerned with the issues debated in this book. Descriptions are derived from materials provided by the organizations. All have publications or information available for interested readers. The list was compiled on the date of publication of the present volume; names, addresses, phone and fax numbers, and e-mail/Internet addresses may change. Be aware that many organizations take several weeks or longer to respond to inquiries, so allow as much time as possible.

Advocates for Abused and Battered Lesbians (AABL)
PO Box 85596, Seattle, WA 98105-9998
(206) 547-8191
e-mail: aabl@isomedia.com • website: http://www.isomedia.com/homes/AABL
AABL provides services for lesbians and their children who are or have been victims of domestic violence. Through community education and outreach, its members encourage communities to recognize and eliminate lesbian battering, homophobia, and misogyny. AABL provides information on intimate abuse, and its website includes stories from survivors of domestic violence.

American Bar Association Commission on Domestic Violence
740 15th St. NW, Washington, DC 20005-1022
(202) 662-1737 • (202) 662-1744 • fax: (202) 662-1594
e-mail: abacdv@abanet.org • website:
http://www.abanet.org/domviol/home.html
The commission researches model domestic violence programs in an effort to develop a blueprint for a national multidisciplinary domestic violence program. The commission provides information on domestic violence law and publishes several books, including *Stopping Violence Against Women: Using New Federal Laws* and *The Impact of Domestic Violence on Your Legal Practice: A Lawyer's Handbook*.

Center for the Prevention of Sexual and Domestic Violence
936 N. 34th St., Suite 200, Seattle, WA 98013
(206) 634-1903 • fax: (206) 634-0115
e-mail: cpsdv@cpsdv.org • website: http://www.cpsdv.org
The center is an interreligious ministry addressing issues of sexual and domestic violence. Its goal is to engage religious leaders in the task of ending abuse through institutional and social change. The center publishes educational videos, the quarterly newsletter *Working Together,* and many books, including *Violence Against Women and Children: A Christian Theological Sourcebook* and *Sexual Violence: The Unmentionable Sin—An Ethical and Pastoral Perspective*.

Family Violence Prevention Fund (FVPF)
383 Rhode Island St., Suite 304, San Francisco, CA 94103-5133
(415) 252-8900 • fax: (415) 252-8991
website: http://www.fvpf.org
FVPF is a national nonprofit organization concerned with domestic violence education, prevention, and public policy reform. It works to improve health care for battered women and to strengthen the judicial system's capacity to respond appropriately to domestic violence cases. The fund sponsored a national education campaign entitled "There's No Excuse for Domestic Vio-

lence" to promote prevention and intervention, and it also publishes information packets on domestic violence such as "You Can Make a Difference! Creative Prevention Strategies" and the survey report *Men Beating Women: Ending Domestic Violence*.

Independent Women's Forum
(800) 224-6000
e-mail: info@iwf.org • website: http://www.iwf.org

The forum is a conservative women's advocacy group that believes in individual freedom and personal responsibility and promotes common sense over feminist ideology. The forum believes that the incidence of domestic violence is exaggerated and that the Violence Against Women Act is ineffective and unjust. It publishes the *Women's Quarterly*.

NOW Legal Defense and Education Fund (NOW LDEF)
99 Hudson St., New York, NY 10013-2871
(212) 925-6635 • fax: (212) 226-1066
website: http://www.nowldef.org

NOW LDEF is a branch of the National Organization for Women (NOW). It is dedicated to the eradication of sex discrimination through litigation and public education. The organization's publications include several legal resource kits on rape, stalking, and domestic violence, as well as information on the Violence Against Women Act.

Office for Victims of Crime Resource Center
810 Seventh St. NW, Washington, DC 20531
(800) 627-6872
website: http://www.ojp.usdoj.gov/ovc

Established in 1983 by the U.S. Department of Justice, the resource center is a primary source of information regarding victim-related issues. It answers questions by using national and regional statistics, research findings, and a network of victim advocates and organizations. The center distributes all Office of Justice Programs publications.

U.S. Department of Justice Violence Against Women Office
10th & Constitution Ave. NW, Room 5302, Washington, DC 20530
National Domestic Violence Hotline: (800) 799-SAFE
fax: (202) 307-3911
website: http://www.usdoj.gov/vawo

The office is responsible for the overall coordination and focus of Department of Justice efforts to combat violence against women. It maintains the National Domestic Violence Hotline and publishes a monthly newsletter. An on-line domestic violence awareness manual is available at the office's website along with press releases, speeches, and the full text of and news about the Violence Against Women Act.

BIBLIOGRAPHY

Books

Raquel Kennedy Bergen	*Wife Rape: Understanding the Response of Survivors and Service Providers*. Thousand Oaks, CA: Sage Publications, 1996.
Valerie Nash Chang	*I Just Lost Myself: Psychological Abuse of Women in Marriage*. Westport, CT: Praeger, 1996.
Jill M. Davies	*Safety Planning with Battered Women: Complex Lives/Difficult Choices*. Thousand Oaks, CA: Sage Publications, 1998.
Donald Alexander Downs	*More Than Victims: Battered Women, the Syndrome Society, and the Law*. Chicago: University of Chicago Press, 1996.
Donald Dutton	*The Batterer: A Psychological Profile*. New York: BasicBooks, 1995.
Raoul Felder and Barbara Victor	*Getting Away with Murder: Weapons for the War Against Domestic Violence*. New York: Simon & Schuster, 1996.
Neil S. Jacobson and John M. Gottman	*When Men Batter Women*. New York: Simon & Schuster, 1998.
Ann Jones	*Next Time, She'll Be Dead: Battering and How to Stop It*. Boston: Beacon Press, 1994.
Ethel Klein and J. Campbell	*Ending Domestic Violence*. Thousand Oaks, CA: Sage Publications, 1997.
Anna Kosof	*Battered Women: Living with the Enemy*. New York: Franklin Watts, 1994.
Robert L. Snow	*Family Abuse: Tough Solutions to Stop the Violence*. New York: Plenum Press, 1997.
Jan Berliner Statman	*The Battered Woman's Survival Guide*. Dallas: Taylor Publications, 1995.
Karen J. Wilson	*When Violence Begins at Home: A Comprehensive Guide to Understanding and Ending Domestic Abuse*. Alameda, CA: Hunter House, 1997.

Periodicals

Kathy Braidhill	"A Deadly Force," *Los Angeles*, October 1997.
Julie Brienza	"Lawmakers Seek to Help Battered Women Get Insurance," *Trial*, April 1996.
Liz Brody	"When Love Hurts," *Shape*, February 1998. Available from PO Box 37207, Boone, IA 50037-2207.
Paul A. Cedar	"Abused Women: How Can the Church Help?" *Moody*, September 1995. Available from 820 N. La Salle Blvd., Chicago, IL 60610.

Patricia Chisolm   "The Scourge of Wife Abuse," *Maclean's*, October 30, 1995.

Felicia Collins Correia   "Domestic Violence Can Be Cured," *USA Today*, November 1997.

Robert C. Davis and   "Domestic Violence Reforms: Empty Promises or
Barbara Smith   Fulfilled Expectations?" *Crime & Delinquency*, October–December 1995.

Barbara Ehrenreich   "Battered Welfare Syndrome," *Time*, April 3, 1995.

Raoul Felder and   "Domestic Violence: Should Victims Be Forced to
Anita Blair   Testify Against Their Will?" *ABA Journal*, May 1996.

Jeanette D. Gardner   "When Home Is a Haven of Hurt," *Moody*, September 1995. Available from 820 N. La Salle Blvd., Chicago, IL 60610.

Mary Geraghty   "Training Nurses to Play a Key Role," *The Chronicle of Higher Education*, September 12, 1997. Available from 1255 23rd St. NW, Washington, DC 20037.

Stephanie B. Goldberg   "Nobody's Victim," *ABA Journal*, July 1996.

Jennifer Gonnerman   "Charlene Meets the Media," *Village Voice*, March 4, 1997. Available from 36 Cooper Square, New York, NY 10003.

George Lardner Jr.   "No Place to Hide," *Good Housekeeping*, October 1997.

Fredrica L. Lehrman   "Discovering the Hidden Tort: Domestic Violence May Provide Grounds for Civil Action Against Abusers," *ABA Journal*, September 1996.

Fredrica L. Lehrman   "Factoring Domestic Violence into Custody Cases," *Trial*, February 1996.

Gerald McOscar   "Slap Your Spouse, Lose Your House," *Women's Quarterly*, Spring 1997. Available from 2111 Wilshire Blvd., Suite 550, Arlington, VA 22201-3057.

Donna Parsons   "Insurance Companies Sock It to Battered Women," *On The Issues*, Summer 1996.

Larry Reynolds   "Fighting Domestic Violence in the Workplace," *HR Focus*, November 1997. Available from PO Box 57969, Boulder, CO 80322-7969.

Bonnie Miller Rubin   "From Battered Wife to Top Cop," *Good Housekeeping*, August 1996.

Julie Gannon Shoop   "Breaking the Cycle of Violence," *Trial*, January 1998.

Charlene Marmer   "Picture This: A Safer Workplace," *Workforce*, February
Solomon   1998. Available from PO Box 55695, Boulder, CO 80322-5695.

INDEX